GET MORE FROM YOUR
DEEP FAT FRYER

GET MORE FROM YOUR
DEEP FAT FRYER

Petra Kuhne

W. Foulsham & Co. Ltd.
London • New York • Toronto • Cape Town • Sydney

W. Foulsham & Company Limited
Yeovil Road, Slough, Berkshire, SL1 4JH

ISBN 0-572-01395-7

Originally published by Falken-Verlag GmbH
Niedernhausen/Ts, West Germany

This English language edition copyright
© W. Foulsham & Co. Ltd 1987

Printed in Great Britain by St Edmundsbury Press Ltd, Bury St Edmunds

CONTENTS

INTRODUCTION

The new deep-frying: super deep-frying

Many cookery books today still exclude recipes for deep-frying. The reasons can probably be explained as the often unpleasant side-effects of deep-frying for domestic purposes – smells that cling to clothes, hair and the whole house; splashing oil which sticks to equipment and clothes and can also be extremely painful. Modern technology, though, and healthy, non-splashing fats have made it possible for you to enjoy only the positive sides of deep-frying. If, for example, you are using the new Tefal Super Deep Fryer, then the food will be lowered into the oil – heated to the correct temperature – from the outside, while the lid remains closed (and it will be taken out in the same way). There is no splashing. The steam has to escape through a 2 cm/1 in thick active coal filter. It will be de-greased and odourless when it gets into the kitchen.

So you can now discover for yourself the age-old Chinese art of deep-frying and prepare the most delicious dishes which are only possible with deep-frying.

A note on health

Correct temperature of the oil is necessary to ensure that the pores of the food close immediately when immersed in the fat. This way no fat can penetrate the food, meaning that the nutritional value, juice, vitamins and taste of the food remain completely intact. The modern Tefal Super Deep Fryer has a double thermostat which means you won't have to feel too worried about consuming excessive amounts of fat – the fat is always at the correct temperature so that the food remains healthy.

Expand your menu

French fries are only the beginning of the new deep-frying. Chips, fish, meat, vegetables, doughnuts, fruit in batter – everything turns out as it should be: wholesome, golden brown on the outside, juicy and cooked on the inside. And everything is odourless, free of splashes and quick! The Tefal Super Deep Fryer can cook more than 1 kg/2 lb chips or a quartered chicken or six slices of fish in one go – in minutes.

Deep-frying is an old Chinese art which modern technology has allowed us to rediscover – without odour, without splashing, versatile and wholesome.

This is what you should look out for: odour filter system (1) with 2 cm/1 in thick active coal filter, hermetic bolting of the lid (2) and comfortable turn-button lowering device (3) (guarantees extreme security from odour and splashing). The double thermostat (4) guarantees problem-free deep-frying (position 1 for vegetables and fish, etc, position 2 for meat, chips and deep frozen food, etc). Control window (5) and timer (6) only with the de luxe model. All these advantages are offered by the Tefal Super Deep Fryer.

Golden rules for using fat and for deep-frying

1. Use only vegetable fats of the highest quality. Special deep-frying fat can be heated to very high temperatures without starting to smoke or splash. Animal fats such as lard, suet, whale or fish oils are not suitable for deep-frying. Don't use butter or margarine.

2. Don't use two different sorts of fat. It could make the fat foamy. Used oil cannot be improved by adding new fat. The new fat would be spoiled in a very short time.

3. Always fill the deep-fryer according to the manufacturer's instructions. A simple deep-frying pot should be one-third filled.

4. There is no hard-and-fast rule about how often you can use your deep-frying fat. This depends on the one hand on what you are deep-frying, on the other hand on how well you are looking after the fat. The colour can give you a good indication: once the oil is starting to turn dark brown, it should be renewed.

Leftover pieces from deep-frying change the fat's colour and will also make it smoke. We therefore recommend you to clear the deep-frying fat regularly of such bits. You'd probably be best using a special filter (e.g. Tefal Special Filter Papers).

5. Only insert the food once the control lamp has switched off which indicates that the fat has reached the correct temperature. (For the Tefal Super Deep Fryer compare the hints on the special instruction leaflet.)

6. Dry the food carefully before lowering it slowly into the deep-fryer (lower the basket of the Tefal Super Deep Fryer slowly from the outside): moisture shortens the life span of the deep-frying fat. Prevent salt from getting into the fat, too.

Leave the deep-frying basket in the lower position in the hot fat if the food is coated with a batter or consists of dough. It will then be able to swim freely, and the result will be better.

7. Don't deep-fry too much in one go! The deep-fried food must be able to swim and in some recipes is not supposed to touch. This is particularly true for deep-frozen food (which hasn't thawed) and especially for croquettes. Deep-fry such deep-frozen food in small batches only, for a larger amount makes the temperature of the fat drop too fast. This in turn means that the food will soak up the oil and won't turn crispy at all.

Allow the deep-fried food to drain properly after deep-frying (basket in top position).

8. You can deep-fry different things one after the other, or next to each

other, e.g. fish next to pastries. The flavours will not be affected.

9. When over-heated, the fat easily self-ignites. Your Tefal Super Deep Fryer is safeguarded against this by its double thermostat. Don't ever leave deep fryers on their own, however.

10. Don't ever walk around with a deep fryer filled with hot fat. If you trip up you can suffer very serious burns. The hermetically-sealed lid of the Tefal Super Deep Fryer offers special protection here, too.

11. If the fat is burning, extinguish the fire by closing the lid. Pull out the plug immediately. Never pour any water into hot or burning oil.

12. Read the manufacturer's instructions carefully. You should give your deep fryer the right care and use it correctly if you want it to last a long time.

13. Cleaning the deep fryer

a. Allow the fat to cool down slightly, then pour it into a metal pot with two handles. To do this, lift off the lid. Wipe the inside clean with absorbent paper. (If necessary use hot water and a mild detergent, but never dip the fryer into water.)

b. Put the basket into the top position and place the fat filter paper in it.

c. Now slowly pour the fat back into the deep fryer. Discard the filter paper.

Tips and hints for the recipes

You will find in the following recipes many delicacies, from starters to pastries to accompany tea or coffee. Since one hardly ever eats a kebab, an escalope or a fried fish without accompaniments, and since some people would miss a piquant or a sweet sauce or a refreshing salad, we have given recipe ideas for these as well. It is easiest to use the spice and seasoning mixes now available everywhere. Many deep-fried dishes taste even better when coated with breadcrumbs, with flour or a savoury or sweet batter.

Coating with breadcrumbs: you will probably already have coated an escalope and you will know that you coat it first with flour, then with beaten egg, and finally with breadcrumbs. You can spice the bread-crumbs by mixing in salt and pepper and any other spices you like. Before inserting the coated food into the deep fryer, allow all excess breadcrumbs to drop off, otherwise they will unnecessarily cloud the fat. If you coat the food with flour only, make sure it is very dry so the flour sticks to it. Turn it over carefully.

Batter: food remains particularly juicy if fried in a batter. When deep-frying with the Tefal Super Deep Fryer please note that the basket will remain in the fat and the food will be lowered straight into the fat. Then continue cooking according to the manufacturer's instructions.

Basic recipe for the batter
150 g/5 oz/1½ cups flour
250 ml/9 fl oz/1 cup + 2 tbsp liquid
Pinch of salt or sugar

As a liquid you have the choice of milk, beer, wine or sparkling wine. You can flavour the batter with rum, brandy or other spirits. If you want to refine the batter, add an egg yolk and leave the batter in a warm place to prove. Finally fold in a stiffly beaten egg white. After half the cooking time, turn all pastries and food deep-fried in batter with a fork.

Abbreviations: tbsp = tablespoon
                tsp = teaspoon

Servings: all the recipes serve 4, unless otherwise stated.

1. STARTERS

DEEP-FRIED CAMEMBERT

INGREDIENTS	Metric	Imperial	American
Camembert half-sections	4	4	4
Flour			
Eggs	2	2	2
Breadcrumbs	60 g	$2\frac{1}{4}$ oz	$\frac{1}{2}$ cup

1. Turn the camembert half-sections first in flour, then in beaten egg and finally in the breadcrumbs. Then coat them again with beaten egg and breadcrumbs. Deep-fry in the hot oil.

Cooking time: 2 minutes

DEEP-FRIED PEARS

INGREDIENTS	Metric	Imperial	American
Pears	4 large	4 large	4 large
Lemon juice	2 tbsp	2 tbsp	2 tbsp
Roquefort cheese	100 g	4 oz	4 oz
Sherry	2 tsp	2 tsp	2 tsp
Flour			
Egg	1	1	1
Breadcrumbs			
Glacé cherries, to garnish			

1. Peel, halve and core the pears. Sprinkle with lemon juice. Beat Roquefort cheese and sherry together until smooth, then use it to fill the pear halves. Dust the edges with flour and put the pears back together again.
2. Roll the pears first in flour, then in the beaten egg, and finally in the breadcrumbs to coat them evenly. Deep-fry the pears in the hot oil. Garnish with glacé cherries.

Cooking time: 4 minutes

FILLED PANCAKES

INGREDIENTS	Metric	Imperial	American
Flour	100 g	4 oz	1 cup
Eggs	3	3	3
Milk	250 ml	9 fl oz	1 cup
Salt			
Margarine			
Cheese (such as Gouda), thin slices	4 large	4 large	4 large
Flour			
Egg yolk	1	1	1
Breadcrumbs			

1. Make a pancake batter from the flour, egg yolks, milk and salt, then fold in egg whites. Divide batter into four portions and bake thin pancakes in a little margarine. Place the cheese slices on top of the pancakes and roll each one up tightly like a Swiss roll.

2. Coat the pancake rolls first with flour, then turn them in the beaten egg yolk, and finally coat with breadcrumbs. Deep-fry the pancake rolls in hot fat. Divide each pancake roll into four pieces and serve with a crisp salad.

Cooking time: 2 minutes

MUSSEL FRITTERS

INGREDIENTS	Metric	Imperial	American
Mussels, canned	200 g	7 oz	7 oz
Flour			
Egg, beaten	1	1	1
White bread	$\frac{1}{2}$ loaf	$\frac{1}{2}$ loaf	$\frac{1}{2}$ loaf

1. Remove the crusts from the bread and grate it for coating. Drain the mussels, then coat them with the flour, beaten egg and breadcrumbs. Deep-fry them in batches until golden brown.

Cooking time: 4 minutes

CHEESE KEBABS IN BATTER

INGREDIENTS	Metric	Imperial	American
White bread, slices	4	4	4
Emmental cheese, thick slices	2	2	2
Salami, slices	8	8	8
Flour	100 g	4 oz	1 cup
Egg	1	1	1
Milk	2 tbsp	2 tbsp	2 tbsp
Salt and pepper			

1. Cut the crusts off the bread and cut the bread into equal-sized squares. Cut cheese and salami into squares. Thread bread, cheese and salami squares alternately on to wooden skewers.

2. Make a batter from the flour, egg, milk and salt and pepper. Dip the kebabs into the batter, then deep-fry in the hot oil and serve immediately.

Cooking time: 3 minutes

SAVOURY DOUGHNUTS

INGREDIENTS	Metric	Imperial	American
Water	250 ml	9 fl oz	1 cup
Salt	1 pinch	1 pinch	1 pinch
Margarine	50 g	2 oz	$\frac{1}{2}$ cup
Flour	125 g	4 $\frac{1}{2}$ oz	1 cup
Eggs	3	3	3
Ham, finely chopped	50 g	2 oz	$\frac{1}{4}$ cup
Cheese, grated	2 tbsp	2 tbsp	2 tbsp
Baking powder	1 tsp	1 tsp	1 tsp

1. Bring the water to the boil, together with the salt and the margarine. Tip all the flour in and stir very quickly until smooth. Leave to cool a little, then stir in the eggs, one at a time. Add the baking powder, grated cheese and chopped ham.

2. Put the dough into a piping bag fitted with a large, even spout and

pipe small heaps on to a slotted spoon. Lower the doughnuts with the spoon into the hot oil and deep-fry until golden brown.

3. Serve with a salad and with wine or beer.

Cooking time: 4 minutes

FILLED SPRING ROLLS

INGREDIENTS	Metric	Imperial	American
Flour	150 g	5 oz	1¼ cups
Water	250 ml	9 fl oz	1 cup
Egg white	1	1	1
Salt			
Cooked pork	100 g	4 oz	4 oz
Garlic powder	1 pinch	1 pinch	1 pinch
Celeriac	40 g	1½ oz	1½ oz
Bamboo sprouts	1 small can	1 small can	1 small can
Chinese cabbage or Savoy cabbage	75 g	3 oz	3 oz
Soy sauce	2 tbsp	2 tbsp	2 tbsp
Salt			
Pepper			

1. Make a thin batter from the flour, water and salt. Whisk egg white until stiff, then fold into the batter. Grease a frying pan and use to bake very thin pancakes. Do not pile them on top of each other.

2. For the filling, cut the meat into thin strips. Peel the celeriac and, together with the rest of the vegetables, chop finely. Heat a little oil in a large frying pan, add the meat with the garlic powder and fry for a few minutes. Add the vegetables and soy sauce and season to taste with salt and pepper.

3. Fry everything together, stirring, until well done. Add a little meat stock and leave to simmer until all the liquid has evaporated. Leave to cool.

4. Place 2 tbsp of the filling on each pancake, then roll them up into parcels so that the filling cannot escape. Heat the oil and deep-fry the spring rolls. Serve as a starter with a green salad.

Cooking time: 4 minutes

CELERIAC APPLE FRITTERS

INGREDIENTS	Metric	Imperial	American
Celeriac	1	1	1
Vinegar water			
Apple	1	1	1
Flour	125 g	$4\frac{1}{2}$ oz	1 cup
Eggs	2	2	2
Beer	125 ml	4 fl oz	$\frac{1}{2}$ cup
Salt and pepper			

1. Peel the celeriac and then cut into $\frac{1}{2}$ cm/$\frac{1}{4}$ in slices. Cook in the vinegar water for about 7 minutes. Peel the apple and cut into $\frac{1}{2}$ cm/$\frac{1}{4}$ in slices.

2. Combine flour, eggs, beer and seasoning for the batter. Dip celeriac and apple slices into the batter, then deep-fry in the hot oil. Turn after 3 minutes, using a fork.

3. Serve as starters on lightly dressed lettuce leaves.

Cooking time: 3 minutes

CHEESE DUMPLINGS

INGREDIENTS	Metric	Imperial	American
Milk	250 ml	9 fl oz	1 cup
Fat	50 g	2 oz	$\frac{1}{4}$ cup
Salt			
Cornflour	50 g	2 oz	$\frac{1}{2}$ cup
Flour	50 g	2 oz	$\frac{1}{2}$ cup
Eggs	2	2	2
Swiss cheese, grated	100 g	4 oz	1 cup

1. Heat the milk with the fat and a little salt. Mix cornflour and flour and tip into the milk mixture in one go. Stir until the mixture becomes one large dumpling. Add and stir in one egg. Leave the mixture to cool slightly, then stir in the second egg and the grated cheese.

2. Dip one teaspoon into the hot oil, then use to form small dumplings from the mixture. Lower into the oil and deep-fry. Keep warm until all dumplings have been cooked. These can be used in soups.

Cooking time: 3 minutes

PRAWN FRITTERS

INGREDIENTS	Metric	Imperial	American
Flour	250 g	9 oz	2¼ cups
Margarine	100 g	4 oz	½ cup
Egg yolks	2	2	2
Cream	2-3 tbsp	2-3 tbsp	2-3 tbsp
Prawns, deep-frozen	250 g	9 oz	2½ cups
Lemon juice			

1. Make a shortcrust pastry from the flour, margarine, egg yolks and cream and chill for 30 minutes. In the meantime, defrost the prawns and sprinkle with lemon juice.

2. Form long rolls from the dough and cut off pieces approximately 2 cm/1 in long. Press a prawn into each piece and form into little balls. Deep-fry in the hot oil until golden brown
Cooking time: 4 minutes

ONION DUMPLINGS

INGREDIENTS	Metric	Imperial	American
Onions	100 g	4 oz	1 cup
Margarine	50 g	2 oz	¼ cup
Oats, rolled	50 g	2 oz	½ cup
Egg	1	1	1
Salt			
Nutmeg			
Parsley			

1. Chop the onions finely. Heat the margarine in a frying pan, add onions and oats and simmer over gentle heat.

2. In a bowl mix egg, salt, nutmeg and parsley. Add the onion mixture. Dip 2 teaspoons into hot oil and use to form small dumplings out of the mixture. Deep-fry the dumplings in batches. These can be used in soups.

Cooking time: 2 minutes

2. POULTRY

VIENNESE BAKED CHICKEN

INGREDIENTS	Metric	Imperial	American
Chicken pieces	4	4	4
Salt			
Pepper			
Flour			
Eggs	1-2	1-2	1-2
Breadcrumbs			
Paprika	$\frac{1}{2}$ tsp	$\frac{1}{2}$ tsp	$\frac{1}{2}$ tsp
Lemon	1	1	1
Parsley			

1. Bone the chicken pieces as far as possible. Season with salt and pepper to taste and leave to stand for a short time. Turn the chicken pieces first in flour, then in beaten egg. Mix the breadcrumbs with the paprika and use to coat the chicken pieces. Deep-fry in hot oil.

2. Drain the chicken pieces and pat dry on absorbent paper. Garnish with lemon slices and parsley.

Cooking time: 15 minutes

POULTRY BALLS

INGREDIENTS	Metric	Imperial	American
White sauce	250 ml	9 fl oz	1 cup
Poultry meat, cooked	200 g	7 oz	7 oz
Eggs	2	2	2
Curry powder			
Lemon juice			
Breadcrumbs			

1. Make the white sauce according to directions and simmer for 2 minutes. Cut the poultry meat into small dices and add to the sauce. Stir

in the eggs and add curry powder and lemon juice to taste. Leave to cool.

2. Form the mixture into small balls and coat them with breadcrumbs. Deep-fry in the hot oil until golden brown. Serve on lightly dressed lettuce leaves.

Cooking time: 2-3 minutes

TURKEY ESCALOPES

INGREDIENTS	Metric	Imperial	American
To serve 2			
Turkey leg, deep-frozen	1	1	1
Celeriac	40g	1½ oz	⅔ cup
Carrot	1	1	1
Leek	1	1	1
Onion	1	1	1
Salty water			
Schnapps			
Flour			
Egg	1	1	1
Salt			
Paprika			
Breadcrumbs			

1. Allow turkey leg to thaw slightly, then cook together with the peeled and chopped celeriac and carrot and the trimmed and sliced leek and the peeled onion in the salty water for about 50 minutes.

2. Separate the cooked leg into even-sized escalopes and sprinkle with schnapps. Beat the egg and season with salt and paprika. Coat the turkey escalopes first with flour, then dip into the beaten egg and finally coat with breadcrumbs. Deep-fry in the hot oil.

3. Serve with chips and cauliflower.

Cooking time: 3-4 minutes

3. KEBABS

SAUSAGES ON A SKEWER

INGREDIENTS	Metric	Imperial	American
Sausage meat	250 g	9 oz	1 cup
Breadcrumbs			
Mixed pickles or olives			

1. Form the sausage–meat into walnut-sized balls. Coat the balls with breadcrumbs and deep-fry them in the hot oil.

2. Put one deep-fried sausage ball and one piece of mixed pickles or one olive on each cocktail stick.

Cooking time: 3 minutes

PORK-MUSHROOM KEBABS

INGREDIENTS	Metric	Imperial	American
Pork escalopes	375 g	13 oz	13 oz
Onions	2	2	2
Tomatoes	2	2	2
Gherkin	1	1	1
Carrot, cooked	1	1	1
Apple	$\frac{1}{2}$	$\frac{1}{2}$	$\frac{1}{2}$
Mushrooms	8	8	8
Salt			
Paprika			

1. Cut the meat into large dice, quarter onions and tomatoes, slice the gherkin and the carrot thickly and cut the apple into large chunks. Trim and wash the mushrooms.

2. Thread all the ingredients on to skewers in a colourful sequence, and deep-fry in the hot oil. Season with salt and paprika and serve.

Cooking time: 3 minutes

LIVER KEBABS

INGREDIENTS	Metric	Imperial	American
Calf's liver	500 g	1 lb	1 lb
Red apples	2	2	2
Pickling onions	3 tbsp	3 tbsp	3 tbsp
Bacon	150 g	5 oz	5 oz
Salt			

1. Cut the liver into large dice and the unpeeled apples into 8 pieces. Thread all the ingredients on to skewers, the bacon rashers rolled up, and deep-fry in the hot oil.

Cooking time: 4 minutes

2. Serve the kebabs with ketchup and French bread.

MEATBALL KEBABS

INGREDIENTS	Metric	Imperial	American
Minced beef	250 g	$\frac{1}{2}$ lb	1 cup
Minced pork	250 g	$\frac{1}{2}$ lb	1 cup
Onions	2	2	2
Garlic	1 clove	1 clove	1 clove
Egg	1	1	1
Tabasco	2 dashes	2 dashes	2 dashes
Salt			
Pepper			
Paprika			
Ketchup			
Gherkins			
Pickled baby corn on the cob			

1. Combine the minced beef and minced pork with the chopped onions, garlic clove, the egg and the seasonings until smooth. Form the mixture into small balls and cook them in the deep fryer.

Cooking time: 6 minutes

2. Thread the cooked meatballs on to skewers alternately with gherkins and baby corn on the cob and stick the skewers into a grapefruit.

HUNGARIAN KEBABS

INGREDIENTS	Metric	Imperial	American
Pork	350 g	12 oz	12 oz
Green pepper	1	1	1
Red pepper	1	1	1
Bacon	50 g	2 oz	2 oz
Onions	2	2	2
Paprika			
Pepper			

1. Cut the meat into 2 cm/1 in even-sized cubes. Core and wash the peppers, then cut them into even-sized pieces. Cut bacon into small pieces, onions into quarters. Thread all the ingredients alternatively on to skewers. Dust with paprika and pepper and deep-fry in the hot oil.

Cooking time: 8 minutes

2. Serve with mashed potato and mixed vegetables.

MOCK CORDON BLEU

INGREDIENTS	Metric	Imperial	American
Belly pork, thin slices	8	8	8
Salt and pepper			
Paprika			
Emmental cheese, slices	2	2	2
Bacon rashers	2	2	2
Flour			
Egg	1	1	1
Breadcrumbs			

1. Cut the rind off the meat, and beat to flatten. Sprinkle with salt, pepper and paprika to taste. Halve the cheese slices and the bacon rashers.

2. Make a sandwich of 1 thin slice of belly pork, $\frac{1}{2}$ cheese slice, $\frac{1}{2}$ bacon rasher and 1 thin slice belly pork, and press together. Secure with cocktail sticks if necessary. Coat first with flour, then with beaten egg and finally with breadcrumbs. Deep-fry in the hot oil.

Cooking time: 4 minutes

SAUSAGE KEBABS

INGREDIENTS	Metric	Imperial	American
German sausages	4	4	4
Pickled cucumbers	2	2	2
Lemon juice			
Bananas	2	2	2
Bacon rashers	4-8	4-8	4-8

1. Cut sausages, cucumbers and lemon-juice-sprinkled bananas into thick slices and thread alternately on to skewers. Deep-fry in the hot oil.

Cooking time: 3 minutes

2. Dust with paprika and serve piping hot with toast.

MILANESE ESCALOPES

INGREDIENTS	Metric	Imperial	American
Pork escalopes	4	4	4
Eggs	2	2	2
Parmesan cheese, grated	6 tbsp	6 tbsp	6 tbsp
Flour	2 tbsp	2 tbsp	2 tbsp
Milk	a little	a little	a little
Salt and pepper			
Tomato sauce	250 ml	9 fl oz	1 cup
Evaporated milk	1 tbsp	1 tbsp	1 tbsp
Sugar	1 pinch	1 pinch	1 pinch
Marjoram	1 pinch	1 pinch	1 pinch

1. Season the pork escalopes with salt and pepper. Make a batter from the eggs, cheese, flour, milk and salt and pepper. Coat the escalopes with the batter, then deep-fry them in the hot oil.

Cooking time: 6 minutes

2. Heat up the tomato sauce and refine with evaporated milk, sugar and marjoram. Serve separately with the Milanese escalopes.

ALMOND ESCALOPES

INGREDIENTS	Metric	Imperial	American
Pork escalopes	4	4	4
Salt and pepper			
Flour			
Egg	1	1	1
Flaked almonds	80 g	3 oz	$\frac{3}{4}$ cup

1. Season the pork escalopes with salt and pepper, then coat with flour. Turn in the beaten egg and then coat with flaked almonds. Press almonds down firmly so they stick. Deep-fry in the hot oil.

Cooking time: 7 minutes

SURPRISE STEAKS

INGREDIENTS	Metric	Imperial	American
Minced beef	250 g	9 oz	$1\frac{1}{4}$ cups
Minced pork	250 g	9 oz	$1\frac{1}{4}$ cups
Bread roll	1	1	1
Egg	1	1	1
Garlic powder			
Mustard	1 tsp	1 tsp	1 tsp
Marjoram			
Salt and pepper			
Pineapple slices, canned	4 small	4 small	4 small
Grated cheese	100 g	4 oz	1 cup
Breadcrumbs	1 tbsp	1 tbsp	1 tbsp

1. Soak the roll and press out. Combine minced meats, roll, egg, garlic powder, mustard and marjoram and season generously with salt and pepper.

2. Divide the mixture into 4 portions and enclose 1 small pineapple slice in each portion. Combine grated cheese and breadcrumbs. Turn the beefsteaks in the breadcrumb mixture, then deep-fry them in the hot oil.

Cooking time: 5-6 minutes

3. Serve with a fresh side salad and French bread.

KEBABS WITH CURRY-BANANA-SAUCE

INGREDIENTS	Metric	Imperial	American
Kidneys	300 g	11 oz	11 oz
Leg of mutton	350 g	12 oz	12 oz
Onions	2	2	2
Peppers	2	2	2
Bacon	150 g	5 oz	5 oz
Curry sauce	500 ml	18 fl oz	$2\frac{1}{4}$ cups
Banana	1	1	1
Flaked almonds			

1. Soak the kidneys in water for about 1 hour, then trim and cut off any skin or tubes. Cut kidneys and leg of mutton into cubes, onions, peppers and bacon into large pieces. Thread all the ingredients alternately on to skewers. Deep-fry in the hot oil.

Cooking time: 4 minutes

2. Heat the curry sauce according to instructions. Cut the banana into thin slices and add to the sauce. Pour the sauce over the skewers and sprinkle with flaked almonds.

3. Serve with mashed potato and a green salad.

SCOTCH EGGS

INGREDIENTS	Metric	Imperial	American
Minced beef	150 g	5 oz	$\frac{3}{4}$ cup
Minced pork	150 g	5 oz	$\frac{3}{4}$ cup
Old roll, soaked and pressed out	1	1	1
Egg	1	1	1
Salt and pepper			
Parsley			
Hard-boiled eggs	2	2	2

1. Make a spicy meat mixture from the ingredients. Shell the eggs and wrap them in the meat mixture. Deep-fry in the hot oil, then cut each Scotch egg in half.

Cooking time: 4 minutes

DEEP-FRIED RISSOLES

INGREDIENTS	Metric	Imperial	American
Minced beef	200 g	7 oz	$\frac{1}{2}$ cup
Minced pork	175 g	6 oz	$\frac{1}{2}$ cup
Celeriac, grated	250 g	9 oz	9 oz
Egg	1	1	1
Breadcrumbs	2 tbsp	2 tbsp	2 tbsp
Salt and pepper			
Thyme			

1. Combine all the ingredients and shape into very flat meatballs. Deep-fry in the hot oil.

Cooking time: 3-4 minutes

2. Serve garnished with tomato wedges and parsley.

MEAT FRITTERS WITH A HOT CHEESE DIP

INGREDIENTS	Metric	Imperial	American
Luncheon meat	600 g	$1\frac{1}{4}$ lb	$1\frac{1}{4}$ lb
Egg	1	1	1
Breadcrumbs	4 tbsp	4 tbsp	4 tbsp
Paprika	1 tsp	1 tsp	1 tsp
Margarine	1 tbsp	1 tbsp	1 tbsp
Onions	4 large	4 large	4 large
Parsley			
Condensed cream of mushroom soup, can	1 small	1 small	1 small
Cheese spread	1 triangle	1 triangle	1 triangle
Sherry	3 tbsp	3 tbsp	3 tbsp
Salt			
Pepper			
Worcestershire sauce			

1. Cut the luncheon meat into thin strips. Beat the egg. Combine the breadcrumbs with the paprika. Coat the meat first with the beaten egg, then with the breadcrumb-paprika mixture. Deep-fry in the hot oil.

Cooking time: 2-3 minutes

2. Melt the margarine and fry the sliced onions in it until translucent, then serve with the meat fritters and the parsley.

3. For the dip, heat the mushroom soup according to instructions, using, however, only half a can of water. Chop the cheese and add to the soup. Cook, stirring, until the cheese has melted. Add the sherry, salt, pepper, and Worcestershire sauce. Keep the dip hot on the table on a hot-plate.

MEATBALL SALAD 'TANGERINE'

INGREDIENTS	Metric	Imperial	American
Minced beef	200 g	7 oz	1 cup
Minced pork	175 g	6 oz	$\frac{3}{4}$ cup
Roll	1	1	1
Egg	1	1	1
Tomato ketchup	2 tbsp	2 tbsp	2 tbsp
Salt and pepper			
Paprika			
Mushrooms, canned	115 g	4 oz	4 oz
Tangerines, canned	115 g	4 oz	4 oz
Pineapple pieces, canned	225 g	8 oz	8 oz
Mayonnaise	100 g	4 oz	1 cup
Mustard	1 tsp	1 tsp	1 tsp
Tangerine juice	2 tbsp	2 tbsp	2 tbsp

1. Soak, then press out the roll. Combine minced meat, roll, egg, tomato ketchup and season with salt, pepper and paprika to taste. Shape mixture into small balls and deep-fry them in the hot oil.

Cooking time: 3-4 minutes

2. Drain the meatballs and leave to cool completely. Drain mushrooms, tangerines and pineapple pieces and add to the meatballs. Stir mayonnaise, mustard and tangerine juice together and season with salt and pepper if necessary. Pour the dressing over the salad and mix everything well. Leave to develop the flavour.

VEAL OLIVES

INGREDIENTS	Metric	Imperial	American
Veal escalopes	4	4	4
Salt			
Paprika			
Ham, slices	4	4	4
Eggs	4	4	4

1. Pat the escalopes until flat, then rub with salt and paprika. Place 1 slice of ham on each escalope, cut off the edges. Place 1 hard-boiled egg in the middle of each ham slice. Roll up the escalopes like a Swiss roll and tie firmly with a piece of string. Deep-fry in the hot oil.

Cooking time: 4-5 minutes

2. Serve with a fresh salad, a piquant gravy and boiled potatoes.

SPICY BEEFSTEAKS

INGREDIENTS	Metric	Imperial	American
Minced beef	250 g	9 oz	$1\frac{1}{4}$ cups
Minced pork	250 g	9 oz	$1\frac{1}{4}$ cups
Bread rolls	2	2	2
Anchovies	4	4	4
Capers	1 tbsp	1 tsbp	1 tbsp
Egg yolks	1-2	1-2	1-2
Cayenne pepper	1 pinch	1 pinch	1 pinch
Flour			
Egg white	1	1	1
Breadcrumbs			

1. Soak the rolls and press out. Combine meat, rolls, chopped anchovies, capers, egg yolk and cayenne pepper until smooth. Using wet hands, shape the mixture into small burgers. Coat the burgers first with flour, then egg white and finally breadcrumbs. Deep-fry in the hot oil.

Cooking time: 3-4 minutes

2. For lunch serve the beefsteaks with boiled potatoes and a fresh salad; for dinner serve with an orange sauce and toast.

MEATBALLS WITH PEAS

INGREDIENTS	Metric	Imperial	American
Minced beef	500 g	1 lb	2 cups
Deep-frozen peas	50 g	2 oz	$\frac{3}{4}$ cup
Onion, chopped	1	1	1
Garlic clove, crushed	1	1	1
Water	75 ml	3 fl oz	6 tbsp
Ginger, ground	$\frac{1}{2}$ tsp	$\frac{1}{2}$ tsp	$\frac{1}{2}$ tsp
Coriander, ground	1 tsp	1 tsp	1 tsp
Caraway seeds, ground	1 tsp	1 tsp	1 tsp
Chilli sauce	1 tbsp	1 tbsp	1 tbsp
Salt			
Turmeric	$\frac{1}{2}$ tsp	$\frac{1}{2}$ tsp	$\frac{1}{2}$ tsp

1. Combine all the ingredients well and season to taste. Shape into little balls and deep-fry in the hot oil.

Cooking time: 4 minutes

PEPPER KEBABS BUDAPEST

INGREDIENTS	Metric	Imperial	American
Pork fillet	250 g	9 oz	9 oz
Pig's liver	250 g	9 oz	9 oz
Streaky bacon	100 g	4 oz	4 oz
Onions	2	2	2
Mushrooms			
Pickled peppers			
Pepper			
Salt			
Paprika			

1. Cut meat and bacon into cubes, quarter the onions and thread alternately with the mushrooms and pieces of pickled peppers on to skewers. Deep-fry in the hot oil.

Cooking time: 2-3 minutes

2. When cooked, dust with pepper, salt and paprika.

MEATBALLS

INGREDIENTS	Metric	Imperial	American
Minced beef	100 g	4 oz	$\frac{L}{4}$ cup
Minced pork	100 g	4 oz	$\frac{L}{4}$ cup
Egg	1	1	1
Salt and pepper			
Onion	1	1	1
Breadcrumbs	2 tbsp	2 tbsp	2 tbsp
Spanish olives	6-8	6-8	6-8

1. Combine all the ingredients to form a spicy mixture. Chop the olives and mix in. Shape into walnut-sized balls and deep-fry in the hot oil.

Cooking time: 4 minutes

DEEP-FRIED LIVER

INGREDIENTS	Metric	Imperial	American
Liver	600 g	$1\frac{L}{4}$ lb	$1\frac{L}{4}$ lb
Salt and paprika			
Oil	2 tbsp	2 tbsp	2 tbsp
Flour	150 g	5 oz	$1\frac{L}{4}$ cups
Beer	225 ml	8 fl oz	1 cup
Oil	1 tbsp	1 tbsp	1 tbsp
Salt	1 pinch	1 pinch	1 pinch
Egg white	2	2	2

1. Skin the liver, then spice it and brush with oil. Leave to marinate for a while. For the batter, combine the flour with the beer, oil and salt and leave to stand for 1 hour. Whisk the egg whites until stiff and fold into the batter. Drain the liver, coat it with the batter and deep-fry in the hot oil.

Cooking time: 3 minutes

2. Serve with mashed potato and fried onion rings. Coat the onion rings with the same beer batter and deep-fry them in the same fat.

4. FISH

DEEP-FRIED EEL

INGREDIENTS	Metric	Imperial	American
Eel	1 large	1 large	1 large
Salt			
Water	300 ml	11 fl oz	$1\frac{1}{3}$ cups
Onion, peeled	1	1	1
Herbs	1 bunch	1 bunch	1 bunch
Milk			
Flour			

1. Have the eel prepared by the fishmonger, then cut it into 5-6 cm/2-2$\frac{1}{2}$ in pieces. Bring the water to the boil with the onion, herbs and salt, add the eel pieces and leave to simmer for about 8 minutes.

2. Drain, pat dry and then dip into milk and coat with flour. Deep-fry in the hot oil.

Cooking time: 4 minutes

DEEP-FRIED FISH BITES

INGREDIENTS	Metric	Imperial	American
Mackerel	500 g	1 lb	1 lb
Flour	300 g	11 oz	$2\frac{3}{4}$ cups
Milk	500 ml	18 fl oz	$2\frac{1}{4}$ cups
Eggs	2	2	2
Nutmeg			
Salt and pepper			

1. Cut the prepared fish into bite-sized pieces and turn in the flour. Make a batter from the remaining flour, milk, eggs, nutmeg and seasoning. Coat the fish bites with the batter and deep-fry in the hot oil until golden brown.

Cooking time: 2-3 minutes

FISH BURGERS

INGREDIENTS	Metric	Imperial	American
Fish trimmings, raw	600 g	1 lb 4 oz	1 lb 4 oz
Salt			
Paprika	1 tsp	1 tsp	1 tsp
Lemon	1	1	1
Capers	2 tsp	2 tsp	2 tsp
Anchovy paste	2 tsp	2 tsp	2 tsp
Bread roll	1	1	1
Egg white	1	1	1
Pickled cucumbers	2	2	2
Flour			

1. Finely chop the fish. Combine with the salt, paprika, juice of the lemon, chopped capers and anchovy paste. Soak and press out the roll and mix into the fish mixture together with the egg white until smooth.

2. Shape into medium-sized balls. Press a piece of pickled cucumber into the middle of each fish ball, then coat them with flour. Deep-fry in the hot oil.

Cooking time: 3-4 minutes

3. Serve with lemon wedges and a fresh salad.

DELICIOUS FISH FINGERS

INGREDIENTS	Metric	Imperial	American
Fish fingers, deep-frozen	1 packet	1 packet	1 packet
Mixed pickles			
Tomato			
Mayonnaise			
Parsley			

1. Deep-fry the fish fingers, without defrosting them first, until golden brown.

Cooking time: 4 minutes

2. Leave to cool, then serve with mixed pickles, tomato wedges, mayonnaise and parsley. French bread makes a good accompaniment.

DEEP-FRIED FISH FILLET WITH BANANAS

INGREDIENTS	Metric	Imperial	American
Deep-frozen fish fillet	400 g	14 oz	14 oz
Lemon juice			
Salt			
Flour			
Bananas	4	4	4
Curry sauce	250 ml	9 fl oz	1 cup

1. Defrost the fish fillet until the flour will coat it well. Sprinkle the fish with lemon juice, salt it, then carefully turn it in the flour to coat. Shake off excess flour. Deep-fry in the hot oil.

Cooking time: 4 minutes

2. Take the fish out and keep warm. Deep-fry the bananas at the same temperature for about 2 minutes, then halve and arrange on top of the fish fillets. Heat the curry sauce and pour over the fish. Serve with a fresh side salad and boiled rice.

FISH STEAKS IN A HERB BATTER

INGREDIENTS	Metric	Imperial	American
Flat fish steaks	4	4	4
Vinegar			
Worcestershire sauce			
Salt			
Dill	1 bunch	1 bunch	1 bunch
Chives	1 bunch	1 bunch	1 bunch
Flour	60 g	$2\frac{1}{4}$ oz	$\frac{1}{2}$ cup
Flour for coating			
Eggs	2	2	2

1. Wash the fish steaks and sprinkle them with vinegar, Worcestershire sauce, salt and chopped herbs. Cover and leave to marinate.

2. In the meantime, make a smooth batter from the flour, eggs and salt. Coat the fish steaks first with flour, then with the batter. Deep-fry in the hot oil.

Cooking time: 8 minutes

DEEP-FRIED SWEET AND SOUR FISH

INGREDIENTS	Metric	Imperial	American
Fillets of fish	750 g	1½ lb	1½ lb
Salt			
Eggs	2	2	2
Cornflour	2 tbsp	2 tbsp	2 tbsp
Wine vinegar	3 tbsp	3 tbsp	3 tbsp
Sweet and sour sauce	200 ml	7 fl oz	1 cup (scant)
Peas, canned	280 g	10 oz	3½ cups
Mushrooms, canned	115 g	4 oz	4 oz

1. Wash the fish and pat dry, then salt it. Combine eggs, cornflour and vinegar to a smooth batter and turn the fish fillet in the batter to coat. Lower into the hot fat in batches and deep-fry.

Cooking time: 4 minutes

2. Drain in the basket and keep warm. Heat the sweet and sour sauce, add the drained peas and mushrooms and simmer until heated through. Pour over the fish.

DEEP-FRIED SEA FRUIT

INGREDIENTS	Metric	Imperial	American
Squid, deep frozen	250 g	9 oz	9 oz
Mussels	250 g	9 oz	9 oz
Shrimps or prawns	125 g	4½ oz	4½ oz
Vinegar			
Salt			
Flour			
Lettuce leaves			

1. Defrost the squid, gut and wash it, then cut into rings. Clean all the sea fruits, sprinkle with vinegar and salt. Dust everything with flour, then deep-fry in the hot oil.

Cooking time: 6-7 minutes

2. Serve on lettuce leaves, with a piquant sauce.

FISH FINGER KEBABS

INGREDIENTS	Metric	Imperial	American
Fish fingers, deep-frozen	1 large packet	1 large packet	1 large packet
Tomatoes	2	2	2
Apple	1	1	1
Onions	2	2	2
Streaky bacon	50 g	2 oz	2 oz

1. Defrost the fish fingers until you can cut them in half. Cut the tomatoes into large pieces. Peel and core the apple and cut into wedges. Slice the onions and the bacon. Thread all the ingredients on to skewers and deep-fry in the hot oil.

Cooking time: 4 minutes

2. Serve a dressed salad with these kebabs.

TROUT IN BATTER

INGREDIENTS	Metric	Imperial	American
Trout, cleaned	4	4	4
Lemon	1	1	1
Fresh mixed herbs			
Salt and pepper			
Water			
Oil	1 tbsp	1 tbsp	1 tbsp
Flour	150 g	5 oz	$1\frac{1}{4}$ cups
Egg whites	2	2	2
Salt	1 pinch	1 pinch	1 pinch

1. Sprinkle the trout with the lemon juice, then rub with the chopped fresh herbs. Season with salt and pepper and leave to stand for a while.

2. For the batter, pour together the oil and the water and stir into the flour in one go. Add a little salt and leave the batter to rise a little in a warm place. Finally whisk the egg white until stiff, then fold into the batter.
Dip the trout into the batter, then deep-fry in the hot oil.

Cooking time: 4 minutes

3. Serve with a potato salad and a piquant sauce.

SOLE WITH GRAPES

INGREDIENTS	Metric	Imperial	American
Sole fillets	4	4	4
Lemon juice			
Salt			
Flour			
Grapes	375 g	13 oz	$2\frac{1}{2}$ cups
Bacon	40 g	$1\frac{1}{2}$ oz	$1\frac{1}{2}$ oz
Margarine	25 g	1 oz	2 tbsp
Cognac	3 tbsp	3 tbsp	3 tbsp

1. Skin, wash and trim the fillets, then sprinkle with salt and coat with flour. Peel the grapes, chop the bacon. Deep-fry the sole fillets in the hot oil and keep warm.

Cooking time: 4-5 minutes

2. Fry the bacon in the margarine until transparent. Add the grapes and fry for a moment, then add the cognac, cover and simmer for about 5 minutes. Serve poured over the sole fillets.

DEEP-FRIED ANCHOVIES

INGREDIENTS	Metric	Imperial	American
Per person:			
Anchovies	4-6	4-6	4-6
Hard-boiled egg yolks	2	2	2
Salt			
Flour			
Parsley			
Lemon slices			

1. Wash the anchovies and trim the larger ones, leave the smaller ones whole. Mash the egg yolks with a fork and combine with a little flour and salt. Turn the drained anchovies in the egg yolk mixture to coat, then deep-fry in the hot oil.

Cooking time: 2-3 minutes

22. Serve on a bed of chopped parsley with lemon slices, together with a piquant sauce.

FISH FILLET IN A BEER BATTER

INGREDIENTS	Metric	Imperial	American
Salmon fillet	750 g	1½ lb	1½ lb
Juice of ½ lemon			
Salt and pepper			
Beer	250 ml	9 fl oz	1 cup
Mustard	1 tsp	1 tsp	1 tsp
Flour	8 heaped tbsp	8 heaped tbsp	8 heaped tbsp
Oil	2 tbsp	2 tbsp	2 tbsp
Sugar	1 tsp	1 tsp	1 tsp
Sauce			
Yoghurt	150 ml	5 fl oz	⅔ cup
Mayonnaise	75 ml	3 fl oz	6 tbsp
Parsley	½ bunch	½ bunch	½ bunch
Dill cucumbers	2	2	2
Hard-boiled egg	1	1	1

1. Wash the fish, sprinkle with the lemon juice, then season. Cut into portion-sized pieces. Put the beer into a bowl, add flour and other ingredients and stir well to mix. Turn the fish pieces in the batter and deep-fry in the hot oil.

Cooking time: 4-5 minutes

2. Make a sauce from the yoghurt, mayonnaise, parsley, chopped cucumbers and chopped egg and serve with the fish. A potato salad would be a good accompaniment.

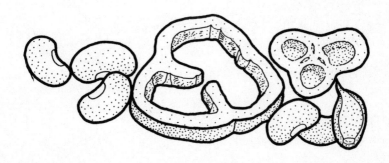

DEEP-FRIED COD

INGREDIENTS	Metric	Imperial	American
Cod or tuna	800 g	1¾ lb	1¾ lb
Lemons	2	2	2
Egg	1	1	1
Milk	2 tbsp	2 tbsp	2 tbsp
Pepper	1 pinch	1 pinch	1 pinch
Salt	½ tsp	½ tsp	½ tsp
Flour			
Parsley			

1. Clean and trim the fish, then cut into 1 cm/½ in slices. Sprinkle the slices with lemon juice and leave to stand for a while. Stir together egg, milk, pepper and salt and beat until frothy. Dip the fish slices into the egg mixture, then coat with flour and deep-fry in the hot oil.

Cooking time: 5 minutes

2. Garnish with lemon wedges and parsley. Serve with a salad and boiled potatoes.

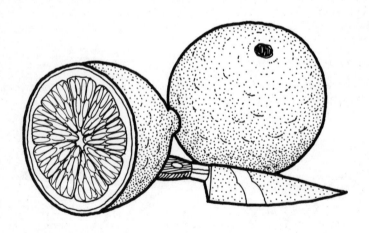

5. POTATO DISHES

CHIPS

INGREDIENTS	Metric	Imperial	American
Potatoes	1 kg	2 lb	2 lb
Salt			
Paprika			

1. Cut the potatoes into even-sized sticks (only then will they brown evenly). Rinse and dry well. Deep-fry in portions in the hot oil, but do not finish browning them.

Cooking time: 4 minutes

2. After cooling, just before serving, deep-fry the chips for a further 2-4 minutes, then season with salt and paprika to taste.

Note: Deep-frozen chips can be deep fried in small portions – not too many at a time (see also 'Golden Rules').

SPICY POTATO BISCUITS

INGREDIENTS	Metric	Imperial	American
Streaky bacon	65 g	$2\frac{1}{2}$ oz	$2\frac{1}{2}$ oz
Onion	1	1	1
Butter	1 tbsp	1 tbsp	1 tbsp
Parsley	1 tbsp	1 tbsp	1 tbsp
Chopped chives	1 tbsp	1 tbsp	1 tbsp
Nutmeg			
Ready-mix potato purée	1 packet	1 packet	1 packet

1. Finely dice the bacon and the onion and sauté in the melted butter. Leave to cool. Add the parsley, chives, nutmeg, bacon and onion to cold water (a quarter less than required on the packet), then stir in the potato purée. Shape the mixture into a roll 4-5 cm/$1\frac{1}{2}$-2 in thick and cut into $1\frac{1}{2}$ cm/$\frac{1}{2}$ in slices. Deep-fry in the hot fat.

Cooking time: 3-4 minutes

POTATO CRISPS

INGREDIENTS	Metric	Imperial	American
Potatoes	1 kg	2 lb	2 lb
Salt			
Paprika			

1. Slice the potatoes finely on a grater, rinse and dry well. Deep-fry in portions in the hot oil, stirring occasionally, until golden brown.

Cooking time: 3-4 minutes

2. Drain the crisps, then season with salt and paprika.

CHANTERELLES FINGERS

INGREDIENTS	Metric	Imperial	American
Water	250 ml	9 fl oz	1 cup
Milk	250 ml	9 fl oz	1 cup
Butter	25 g	1 oz	2 tbsp
Salt			
Ready-mix potato purée	1 packet	1 packet	1 packet
Eggs	2	2	2
Onion	1 small	1 small	1 small
Butter	25 g	1 oz	2 tbsp
Chanterelles, can	1 small	1 small	1 small
Salt			
Pepper			
Parsley			
Golden breadcrumbs			

1. Bring the water, the milk and the butter to the boil and stir in the potato purée, removing the pan from the heat. Add 1 egg. Dice the onion, gently fry in the butter and briefly sauté the chanterelles in it as well. Season with salt and pepper and add parsley. Add the chanterelles to the purée.

2. Shape the mixture into a roll and cut off pieces 2 cm/$\frac{3}{4}$ in long. Beat 1 egg and coat the fingers in it, then in the breadcrumbs. Deep-fry in the hot oil.

Cooking time: 4 minutes

HERBED POTATO BISCUITS

INGREDIENTS	Metric	Imperial	American
Ready-mix potato purée	1 packet	1 packet	1 packet
Water	250 ml	9 fl oz	1 cup
Milk	250 ml	9 fl oz	1 cup
Salt			
Egg yolk	1	1	1
Flour	1 tbsp	1 tbsp	1 tbsp
Herbs, chopped	3 tbsp	3 tbsp	3 tbsp
Nutmeg			

1. Prepare the potato purée according to instructions using however, only 250 ml/9 fl oz/1¾ cups each of milk and water. Add the egg yolk and the flour and combine well, then add the herbs and some nutmeg. Shape the mixture into a roll 6 cm/2½ in thick and cut into thin slices. Deep-fry in the hot oil until golden brown.

Cooking time: 4 minutes

POTATO FINGERS

INGREDIENTS	Metric	Imperial	American
Ready-mix potato purée	1 packet	1 packet	1 packet
Water	375 ml	12 fl oz	1½ cups
Salt			
Ground nutmeg			
Butter or margarine	30 g	1 oz	2 tbsp
Egg yolks	2	2	2
Egg white			
Breadcrumbs			

1. Prepare the potato purée according to the instructions, using only 375 ml/12 fl oz/1½ cups, however. Spice with nutmeg. Stir in the butter or margarine and the egg yolks. Shape the mixture into rolls 2 cm/¾ in thick and 5 cm/2 in long. Turn in the egg white, then in the bread-crumbs, and deep-fry in small portions only in the hot oil. The frozen potato fingers should swim freely in the fat and not touch each other. (See 'Golden Rules'.)

Cooking time: 3-4 minutes

CHEESE FINGERS

INGREDIENTS	Metric	Imperial	American
Ready-mix potato purée	1 packet	1 packet	1 packet
Water	375 ml	13 fl oz	$1\frac{3}{4}$ cups
Salt			
Nutmeg			
Butter or margarine	25 g	1 oz	2 tbsp
Egg yolks	2	2	2
Egg white			
Cheese, grated			

1. Prepare the potato purée according to the instructions, using, however, only 375 ml/13 fl oz/$1\frac{3}{4}$ cups water. Spice with nutmeg, add the butter or margarine and the egg yolks. Shape the mixture into rolls about 2 cm/$\frac{3}{4}$ in thick and cut into pieces 4-5 cm/$1\frac{1}{2}$-2 in long. Coat the fingers in egg white, then in grated cheese and deep-fry in the hot oil.

Cooking time: 3-4 minutes

ALMOND FINGERS

1. Prepare like potato or cheese fingers, but turn in white or toasted breadcrumbs that have been mixed with grated almonds.

HAM BISCUITS

INGREDIENTS	Metric	Imperial	American
Ham	100 g	4 oz	4 oz
Onion	1	1	1
Water	375 ml	13 fl oz	$1\frac{3}{4}$ cups
Ready-mix potato purée	1 packet	1 packet	1 packet

1. Finely dice the ham and the onion. Pour the water over them, then stir in the purée. Shape the mixture into a roll 5 cm/2 in thick and cut into slices about 1 cm/$\frac{1}{2}$ in thick. Shape the biscuits into ovals and deep-fry in the hot fat.

Cooking time: 3-4 minutes

2. These ham biscuits go well if served with roast veal and cucumber salad.

POTATO PASTA

INGREDIENTS	Metric	Imperial	American
Ready-mix potato purée	1 packet	1 packet	1 packet
Water	375 ml	13 fl oz	1¾ cups
Salt			
Pepper			

1. Prepare the potato purée according to the instructions using how-ever, only 375 ml/13 fl oz/1¼ cups water. Season to taste with salt and pepper. Shape the purée into a roll about 2 cm/¾ in thick and cut into pieces 5-6 cm/2-2½ in long. Deep-fry in the hot oil.

Cooking time: 3-4 minutes

POTATO-SEAFOOD-DUMPLINGS WITH CURRY SAUCE

INGREDIENTS	Metric	Imperial	American
Ready-mix potato purée	1 packet	1 packet	1 packet
Emmental cheese, grated	100 g	4 oz	1 cup
Shrimps	150 g	5 oz	5 oz
Dillweed	1 tbsp	1 tbsp	1 tbsp
Ready-mix curry sauce	1 packet	1 packet	1 packet
Mayonnaise	1 tbsp	1 tbsp	1 tbsp

1. Prepare the purée according to the instructions, using a quarter less water than required. Add the cheese, shrimps and chopped dill weed and combine well. Then, using a spoon, shape dumplings and deep-fry them in the hot oil. Drain on paper towels and serve.

Cooking time: 4 minutes

2. Prepare the sauce according to the instructions. Stir in the mayonnaise and serve with the dumplings.

6. VEGETABLES

CUCUMBER SANDWICHES

INGREDIENTS	Metric	Imperial	American
Cucumber	$\frac{1}{2}$	$\frac{1}{2}$	$\frac{1}{2}$
Salt and pepper			
Flour			
Sausage-meat	200 g	7 oz	1 cup
Egg	1	1	1
Breadcrumbs			

1. Cut the cucumber into 16 slices, season with salt and pepper and leave for some time. Then dry the slices and turn in flour.

2. Divide the sausage-meat into 8 parts, shape into balls and place between 2 cucumber slices, then press together well. Turn in the beaten egg, then in the breadcrumbs and deep-fry in the hot oil.

Cooking time: 2-3 minutes

3. Serve on toast with ketchup or with pasta.

BAKED CHICORY WITH HAM

INGREDIENTS	Metric	Imperial	American
Chicory	4	4	4
Salt			
Ham, slices	4	4	4
Cheese (such as Chester), slices	4	4	4
Flour			
Egg	1	1	1
Breadcrumbs			

1. Wash the chicory, cut off the bitter stem and tie the heads with thread. Parboil in salted water for 5-10 minutes and drain well. Remove the threads.

2. Wrap each head of chicory in cheese, then in ham and roll together. Coat with flour, then with the beaten egg and finally with breadcrumbs. Deep-fry in the hot oil.

Cooking time: 3 minutes

3. Serve with a fresh salad.

BAKED LEEKS

INGREDIENTS	Metric	Imperial	American
Leeks	8	8	8
Salt			
Flour			
Egg	1	1	1
Milk			
Breadcrumbs			

1. Trim the leeks to about 15 cm/6 in, wash well and boil in salted water until nearly tender. Drain well, then turn in the flour, in the egg beaten with some milk, and finally in the breadcrumbs. Deep-fry in hot oil.

Cooking time: 4-5 minutes

BAKED MUSHROOMS

INGREDIENTS	Metric	Imperial	American
Mushrooms	250 g	9 oz	9 oz
Flour	125 g	$4\frac{1}{2}$ oz	$1\frac{1}{4}$ cups
Egg	1	1	1
Salt			
Beer	125 ml	4 fl oz	$\frac{1}{2}$ cup
Lettuce, to garnish			

1. Trim and wash the mushrooms, then dry well. Make a pancake batter from the flour, egg, salt and beer, turn the mushrooms in it, using 2 forks, and deep-fry in 2 portions in the hot oil.

Cooking time: 6 minutes

2. Arrange on lettuce leaves and serve with a piquant sauce.

BAKED BRUSSELS SPROUTS

INGREDIENTS	Metric	Imperial	American
Brussels sprouts	750 g	1½ lb	1½ lb
Salt			
Flour	125 g	4½ oz	1 cup
Cheese (such as Chester), grated	100-125 g	4-4½ oz	1 cup
Egg	1	1	1
Water	125 ml	4 fl oz	½ cup

1. Boil the sprouts in salted water until nearly tender, then drain well. In the meantime, prepare a heavy batter from the flour, salt, 30 g/1 oz/⅓ cup cheese, egg and water.

2. Dip a few sprouts into the batter, coat well all round, then deep fry in the hot oil. Remove with a slotted spoon and keep warm until all sprouts are done. Sprinkle with the remaining cheese and serve hot.

Cooking time: 5 minutes

3. Serve with ham, fried eggs or scrambled eggs.

BAKED AUBERGINES WITH TOMATOES

INGREDIENTS	Metric	Imperial	American
Aubergines	3	3	3
Salt	1 pinch	1 pinch	1 pinch
Lemon juice			
Flour	125 g	4½ oz	1 cup
Baking powder	½ tsp	½ tsp	½ tsp
Egg	1	1	1
Milk	125 ml	4 fl oz	½ cup
Tomatoes	500 g	1 lb	1 lb
Onions	2	2	2
Green pepper	1	1	1
Oil	3 tbsp	3 tbsp	3 tbsp
Vinegar	2 tbsp	2 tbsp	2 tbsp
Pepper			

1. Peel the aubergines and cut into slices 1 cm/$\frac{1}{2}$ in thick. Sprinkle with salt and lemon juice. Place the flour and baking powder in a bowl. Beat the egg and milk with the salt and slowly add to the flour, stirring until smooth. Pat the aubergine slices dry, turn in the batter and deep-fry until golden.

Cooking time: 4-6 minutes

2. Slice the tomatoes and onions and dice the green pepper. Combine the oil and vinegar and season to taste. Then pour over the salad. Serve with the aubergine fritters.

BAKED SALSIFY

INGREDIENTS	Metric	Imperial	American
Salsify	1 kg	2 lb	2 lb
Vinegar water			
Lemon	$\frac{1}{2}$	$\frac{1}{2}$	$\frac{1}{2}$
Salt			
Flour	1 tbsp	1 tbsp	1 tbsp
For the batter:			
Flour	150 g	5 oz	$1\frac{1}{4}$ cups
Eggs, separated	2	2	2
Beer	125 ml	4 fl oz	$\frac{1}{2}$ cup
Salt			
Sugar			
Lard	1 tbsp	1 tbsp	1 tbsp

1. Clean the salsify, cut into pieces and immediately cover with vinegar water. Bring water with lemon juice, salt and flour to the boil, add the salsify and cook for 30 minutes until tender. The salsify must be covered with water.

2. Combine the flour, egg yolks and beer to make a smooth batter, adding a little salt and sugar. Whisk the egg whites to form stiff peaks and fold under the batter. Finally stir in the melted lard.
Dry the salsify, turn in flour and then in the batter and deep-fry in portions in the hot oil.

Cooking time: 4 minutes

3. Serve with tomato sauce as side dish with meat dishes.

STUFFED ONIONS

INGREDIENTS	Metric	Imperial	American
Onions	8	8	8
Salt			
Sausage-meat	200 g	7 oz	1 cup
Flour			

1. Peel the onions and boil in salted water for 10-15 minutes. Drain, then cut them in halves lengthways and remove the inner leaves.

2. Divide the sausage-meat into 8 portions and press 1 portion into half of each onion. Press the cut side of the other onion halves into flour and push over a stuffed half.

3. Thread the stuffed onions on to little wooden skewers, turn in flour and deep-fry in hot oil. Arrange on boiled rice. Turn the removed onion parts in flour and deep-fry, then serve with the stuffed onions. They can also be used in soups.

Cooking time: 5-6 minutes

VEGETABLE PLATTER

INGREDIENTS	Metric	Imperial	American
Cauliflower	1 small	1 small	1 small
Haricot beans	250 g	9 oz	1 cup
Fennel	2	2	2
Salt			
Carrots	250 g	9 oz	9 oz
Flour for coating			
Egg	1	1	1
Breadcrumbs			

1. Parboil the cauliflower florets for 5 minutes, the beans and fennel for 10 minutes in salted water. Drain well, then pat dry with a paper towel. Cut the carrots into little sticks. Deep-fry the vegetables, one after the other, in the hot oil.

Cooking time: Carrots 4-6 minutes; cauliflower and beans 2 minutes

2. Halve the fennel, turn in the flour, then in the beaten egg and finally in the breadcrumbs and deep-fry for 4 minutes.

ONION FRITTERS

INGREDIENTS	Metric	Imperial	American
Onions, diced	300 g	11 oz	11 oz
Flour	3 tbsp	3 tbsp	3 tbsp
Eggs	3	3	3
Salt			
Marjoram			

1. Combine the onions with the flour and the eggs, and add seasoning and herbs to taste. Using a tablespoon, cut off small fritters and place into the hot oil.

Cooking time: 3-4 minutes

2. Serve with potato salad.

CABBAGE WEDGES

INGREDIENTS	Metric	Imperial	American
White cabbage	1	1	1
Salted water			
Tomato ketchup	$\frac{1}{2}$ bottle	$\frac{1}{2}$ bottle	$\frac{1}{2}$ bottle
Caraway seeds	$\frac{1}{2}$ tsp	$\frac{1}{2}$ tsp	$\frac{1}{2}$ tsp
Flour			
Eggs	1-2	1-2	1-2
Golden breadcrumbs			

1. Blanch the trimmed cabbage with salted water and leave to cool completely. Combine the ketchup and the caraway. Cut the cabbage into quarters and, if necessary, halve the quarters again.

2. Spread the ketchup mixture on the cabbage pieces, then turn them first in flour, then in the beaten egg(s) and finally in the breadcrumbs. Then deep-fry in the hot oil.

Cooking time: 4 minutes

7. SWEET DESSERTS

QUARK FINGERS

INGREDIENTS	Metric	Imperial	American
Quark	500 g	1 lb	1 lb
Potatoes, boiled and grated	250 g	9 oz	9 oz
Flour	40 g	1½ oz	⅓ cup
Eggs	2	2	2
Sugar	50 g	2 oz	¼ cup

1. Stir the quark smooth, then combine with the remaining ingredients. Shape little fingers and deep-fry in hot oil until golden brown.

Cooking time: 3-4 minutes

2. Serve with stewed plums.

FRUIT SLICES

INGREDIENTS	Metric	Imperial	American
Fruit preserve			
White bread, slices	6	6	6
Cream	125 ml	4 fl oz	½ cup
Vanilla essence	a few drops	a few drops	a few drops
Egg	1	1	1
Toasted breadcrumbs			
Sugar			
Cinnamon			

1. Spread the jam thickly on the bread slices and place them together as sandwiches. Cut into strips 2 cm/¾ in wide. Season the cream with vanilla essence and pour over the bread strips. Leave to soak for 1 hour.

2. Turn the strips first in the beaten egg, then in the breadcrumbs, and deep-fry in the hot oil. After draining, sprinkle with sugar and cinnamon.

Cooking time: 3 minutes

SWEET PEARS

INGREDIENTS	Metric	Imperial	American
Pears	4 large	4 large	4 large
Lemon juice	2 tbsp	2 tbsp	2 tbsp
Marzipan	75 g	3 oz	3 oz
Cherry brandy	1-2 tbsp	1-2 tbsp	1-2 tbsp
Flour			
Egg	1	1	1
Breadcrumbs			

1. Peel and halve the pears (do not remove the stalk), cut out the core and sprinkle with lemon juice. Combine the marzipan with the cherry brandy and fill the pear halves with this mixture. Dust the edges with flour, then put the pears back together again. Roll the pears in flour, then in the beaten egg, and finally in the breadcrumbs. Deep-fry in hot oil until golden brown.

Cooking time: 6 minutes

RICE BALLS

INGREDIENTS	Metric	Imperial	American
Rice	100 g	4 oz	$\frac{1}{2}$ cup
Milk	1 pint	1 pint	2 cups
Sugar	75 g	3 oz	$\frac{1}{3}$ cup
Vanilla essence	a few drops	a few drops	a few drops
Egg yolks	2	2	2
Toasted breadcrumbs			
Sugar			

1. Prepare a thick rice pudding from the rice, milk, sugar and vanilla essence. Leave to cool slightly, then stir in the egg yolks. Spread on a platter and leave to cool.

2. Knead the mixture well, then shape little balls, turn them in the breadcrumbs, pressing them on well, and deep-fry in the hot oil. Drain, then sprinkle with sugar.

Cooking time: 2-3 minutes

3. Serve with a wine cream sauce.

FRUIT IN RUM-BATTER

INGREDIENTS	Metric	Imperial	American
Milk	250 ml	9 fl oz	1 cup + 2 tbsp
Rum	2 small glasses	2 small glasses	2 small glasses
Salt	1 pinch	1 pinch	1 pinch
Sugar	2 tbsp	2 tbsp	2 tbsp
Flour	250 g	9 oz	2¼ cups
Baking powder	1 tsp	1 tsp	1 tsp
Oil	2 tbsp	2 tbsp	2 tbsp
Pineapple, can	½	½	½
Peaches, can	½	½	½

1. Stir the milk with the rum, salt and sugar. Combine the flour and the baking powder and add to the milk mixture with the oil. Stir well. Drain the pineapple and peaches, pat dry with a paper towel and, using a fork, dip in the batter. Deep-fry in the hot oil.

Cooking time: 2-4 minutes

2. Sprinkle the fruit with sugar and cinnamon or serve with a warm fruit sauce.

BAKED PLUM DUMPLINGS

INGREDIENTS	Metric	Imperial	American
Water	250 ml	9 fl oz	1 cup + 2 tbsp
Salt			
Fat	40 g	1½ oz	2 tbsp
Flour	150 g	5 oz	1¼ cups
Eggs	2	2	2
Blue plums	18	18	18
Sugar cubes	18	18	18
Ground nuts			
Icing sugar			

1. Bring the water, salt and fat to the boil, pour in the flour and stir until the dough easily comes off the base of the pan. Remove the pan from the heat and slowly stir in the eggs. Leave to cool, then make the dough into a thick roll and cut into 18 slices.

2. Wash and stone the plums, then fill each one with a sugar cube. Place them on to the dough slices and shape into dumplings. Deep-fry in hot oil until golden brown.

Cooking time: 3-5 minutes

3. Sprinkle with grated nuts and icing sugar and serve hot.

BAKED PUMPKIN

INGREDIENTS	Metric	Imperial	American
Water	250 ml	9 fl oz	1 cup + 2 tbsp
Vinegar	250 ml	9 fl oz	1 cup + 2 tbsp
Sugar	100 g	4 oz	$\frac{1}{2}$ cup
Ground ginger	1 tsp	1 tsp	1 tsp
Pumpkin	1 kg	2 lb	2 lb
Flour	125 g	$4\frac{1}{2}$ oz	$1\frac{1}{4}$ cups
Egg	1	1	1
Salt	1 pinch	1 pinch	1 pinch
Vanilla essence	a few drops	a few drops	a few drops
Sugar			

1. Bring the water with the vinegar, sugar and ginger to the boil. In the meantime, cut the pumpkin into pieces the size of a finger, then pour the hot liquid over them. Cover and leave to cool.

2. Combine the flour, egg, salt, vanilla essence and 125 ml/4 fl oz $\frac{1}{2}$ cup of the liquid and dip the well-drained pumpkin pieces into the batter. Deep-fry in 5 portions in the hot oil. Drain well, then turn in sugar. Serve warm or cold.

Cooking time: 3 minutes

BAKED SLICES OF PEAR

INGREDIENTS	Metric	Imperial	American
Pears, not too hard	500 g	1 lb	1 lb
Lemon juice	a little	a little	a little
Flour for coating			
Evaporated milk	1 tbsp	1 tbsp	1 tbsp
Egg	1	1	1
Desiccated coconut	125 g	$4\frac{1}{2}$ oz	1 cup

1. Peel the pears, then slice them lengthways and sprinkle with lemon juice. Turn the slices first in flour, then in evaporated milk, in the beaten egg, and finally in the desiccated coconut. Deep-fry in portions in the hot oil.

Cooking time: 2-3 minutes

BAKED CHERRIES

INGREDIENTS	Metric	Imperial	American
Flour	70 g	3 oz	$\frac{3}{4}$ cup
Salt	1 pinch	1 pinch	1 pinch
Egg yolk	1	1	1
Sugar	1 tbsp	1 tbsp	1 tbsp
Lemon, grated rind	$\frac{1}{2}$	$\frac{1}{2}$	$\frac{1}{2}$
Single cream	125 ml	4 fl oz	$\frac{1}{2}$ cup
Cherries with stalks	500 g	1 lb	1 lb
Sugar cubes			
Cherry brandy			
Icing sugar			

1. Combine the flour, salt, egg yolk, sugar, lemon rind and cream to make a smooth batter. Stone the cherries from the tip, do not remove the stalk. Soak the sugar cubes in the cherry brandy and fill each cherry with half a sugar cube. Then dip 8-10 cherries into flour, then into the batter and quickly deep-fry until golden brown. Make sure the cherries do not stick together. Drain, then dust with icing sugar.

Cooking time: 2-3 minutes

BANANA BALLS

INGREDIENTS	Metric	Imperial	American
Bananas	2	2	2
Sugar	80 g ·	3 oz	$\frac{1}{3}$ cup
Flour	100 g	4 oz	1 cup
Desiccated coconut	125 g	$4\frac{1}{2}$ oz	1 cup
Vanilla essence	a few drops	a few drops	a few drops
Cointreau	1-2 tbsp	1-2 tbsp	1-2 tbsp
Baking powder	$\frac{1}{4}$ tsp	$\frac{1}{4}$ tsp	$\frac{1}{4}$ tsp

1. Mash the bananas with a fork and combine with the remaining ingredients, leaving some desiccated coconut for coating. Using a teaspoon, cut off little balls and deep-fry in the hot oil. Turn in the reserved coconut.

Cooking time: 3 minutes

DEEP-FRIED MELON WEDGES

INGREDIENTS	Metric	Imperial	American
Honeydew melon	750 g	$1\frac{1}{2}$ lb	$1\frac{1}{2}$ lb
Sugar	100 g	4 oz	$\frac{1}{2}$ cup
Rum	125 ml	4 fl oz	$\frac{1}{2}$ cup
Flour for coating			
Egg	1	1	1
Vanilla flavouring	a few drops	a few drops	a few drops
Sugar for coating			

1. Peel the melon and cut into wedges 1 cm/$\frac{1}{2}$ in thick. Place flat in a large, shallow dish, sprinkle with sugar and rum and leave to soak for at least 1 hour, then pour off the juices.

2. Combine the flour, egg, 125 ml/4 fl oz/$\frac{1}{2}$ cup of the juices and vanilla flavouring to make a thick batter. Turn the melon wedges in flour, then in the batter and deep-fry in portions in the hot oil.

Cooking time: 3-4 minutes

3. Sprinkle with sugar and serve hot. Do not lay the wedges on top of each other, as they will get soggy.

APPLE FRITTERS IN CREAMY PASTRY

INGREDIENTS	Metric	Imperial	American
Margarine	30 g	1 oz	2 tbsp
Sugar	60 g	$2\frac{1}{4}$ oz	$\frac{1}{3}$ cup
Vanilla essence	a few drops	a few drops	a few drops
Eggs, separated	2	2	2
Flour	125 g	$4\frac{1}{2}$ oz	$1\frac{1}{4}$ cups
Single cream	125 ml	4 fl oz	$\frac{1}{2}$ cup
Ground nuts	25 g	1 oz	$\frac{1}{3}$ cup
Rum	2 tbsp	2 tbsp	2 tbsp
Apples	3	3	3
Flour, for coating			
Icing sugar			

1. Whisk the margarine, sugar, vanilla essence and egg yolks until creamy, then add flour and cream, alternating, and finally the nuts and the rum. Fold in the stiffly beaten egg whites.

2. Core and peel the apples, slice them thickly and coat the slices with flour, then dip into the batter. They must be covered completely. Deep-fry 2-3 fritters at a time in the hot oil, drain and dust with icing sugar. They taste good both hot and cold.

Cooking time: 4 minutes

BANANAS IN SHORTCRUST PASTRY

INGREDIENTS	Metric	Imperial	American
Flour	300 g	11 oz	$1\frac{1}{3}$ cups
Baking powder	1 tsp	1 tsp	1 tsp
Sugar	100 g	4 oz	$\frac{1}{2}$ cup
Vanilla essence	a few drops	a few drops	a few drops
Eggs	2	2	2
Margarine	60 g	$2\frac{1}{2}$ oz	$\frac{2}{3}$ cup
Water, if necessary	1 tbsp	1 tbsp	1 tbsp
Bananas	4	4	4
Icing sugar			

1. Combine the flour, baking powder, sugar, vanilla essence, eggs and flaked margarine, and water if necessary, to make a smooth pastry, then chill for some time. Roll out the pastry and cut into 8 rectangles, the length of the bananas.

2. Peel the bananas and cut in half lengthways, wrap each half in a pastry rectangle and firmly press the edges together. Bake in hot oil until golden brown. Drain, sprinkle with icing sugar and serve hot or cold.

Cooking time: 6-8 minutes

TIPSY APPLE DOUGHNUTS

INGREDIENTS	Metric	Imperial	American
Apples	3	3	3
Rum or brandy	1 tbsp	1 tbsp	1 tbsp
Water	250 ml	9 fl oz	1 cup + 2 tbsp
Condensed milk	3 tbsp	3 tbsp	3 tbsp
Salt	1 pinch	1 pinch	1 pinch
Egg yolk	1	1	1
Flour	200 g	7 oz	$1\frac{3}{4}$ cups
Baking powder	1 good pinch	1 good pinch	1 good pinch
Egg white, beaten	1	1	1
Sugar			
Cinnamon			

1. Peel the apples, slice them thickly, then cut out the core. Sprinkle them on a plate with rum or brandy, cover and leave to soak for 15 minutes. Combine the lukewarm water with milk, salt and the egg yolk, then add the flour and the baking powder. Finally fold in the egg white. The batter should be very thick. Dip the apple slices in the batter, then immediately deep-fry in hot oil.

2. Drain, sprinkle with sugar and cinnamon, and serve.

Cooking time: 4-6 minutes

8. BISCUITS AND CAKES

ALMOND-FLAVOURED TREATS

INGREDIENTS	Metric	Imperial	American
Margarine	100 g	4 oz	$\frac{1}{2}$ cup
Sugar	100 g	4 oz	$\frac{1}{2}$ cup
Lemon, grated rind	1	1	1
Eggs	3	3	3
Cornflour	100 g	4 oz	1 cup
Flour	300 g	11 oz	$2\frac{3}{4}$ cups
Ground almonds	50 g	2 oz	$\frac{1}{2}$ cup
Baking powder	1 tsp	1 tsp	1 tsp
Rum	1 tbsp	1 tbsp	1 tbsp
Icing sugar			

1. Combine the ingredients to make a smooth dough, adding the rum at the very end. Leave to chill for 1 hour.

2. Roll out the dough, then cut out 2.5 cm/1 in wide almond shapes. Deep-fry the treats in the hot oil. After draining, dust with icing sugar.

Cooking time: 3 minutes

WAFFLES

INGREDIENTS	Metric	Imperial	American
Flour	125 g	$4\frac{1}{2}$ oz	$1\frac{1}{4}$ cups
Sugar	2 tsp	2 tsp	2 tsp
Salt	1 pinch	1 pinch	1 pinch
Eggs	2	2	2
Milk	125 ml	4 fl oz	$\frac{1}{2}$ cup
Icing sugar			

1. Combine the ingredients to make a smooth pancake batter.

2. Heat the waffle iron in the hot oil. As soon as the oil is hot enough, dip the iron into the batter — the top must not be immersed — and deep-fry the waffles in the hot oil. Drain.

Cooking time: 4-6 minutes

3. Before serving, dust with icing sugar.

DOUGHNUTS

INGREDIENTS	Metric	Imperial	American
Margarine	60 g	$2\frac{1}{2}$ oz	$\frac{2}{3}$ cup
Salt	1 pinch	1 pinch	1 pinch
Sugar	200 g	7 oz	$\frac{3}{4}$ cup
Eggs	2	2	2
Evaporated milk	4 tbsp	4 tbsp	4 tbsp
Flour	500 g	2 lb 2 oz	$8\frac{1}{2}$ cups
Baking powder	3 tsp	3 tsp	3 tsp
Milk	125 ml	4 fl oz	$\frac{1}{2}$ cup
Icing sugar			

1. Whisk the margarine until creamy, then add alternately salt, sugar and eggs and stir until the sugar has dissolved. Add the evaporated milk, and then alternately the flour, the baking powder and the milk.

2. Transfer the mixture to a piping bag with a large nozzle and pipe circles, 6 cm/$2\frac{1}{2}$ in diameter, on to greaseproof paper that has been dipped into fat. Carefully glide the rings from the paper into the hot oil and bake.

Cooking time: 4 minutes

3. Serve dusted with icing sugar.

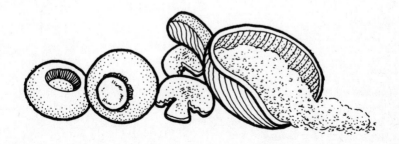

SEMOLINA BEIGNETS

INGREDIENTS	Metric	Imperial	American
Semolina	100 g	4 oz	1 cup
Sugar	50 g	2 oz	$\frac{1}{4}$ cup
Milk	500 ml	18 fl oz	$2\frac{1}{4}$ cups
Cinnamon	1 piece	1 piece	1 piece
Lemon rind	2	2	2
Butter	1 tbsp	1 tbsp	1 tbsp
Oil	1 tbsp	1 tbsp	1 tbsp
Egg	1	1	1
Breadcrumbs			
Sugar			
Cinnamon			

1. Cook the semolina with the sugar, milk, cinnamon, lemon rind and butter. Brush a piece of greaseproof paper or baking foil with oil and spread the semolina evenly on it. Leave to cool.

2. Cut the 'cake' in thin, long pieces, coat them with beaten egg and breadcrumbs and deep-fry them until golden brown.

Cooking time: 3 minutes

3. Drain, sprinkle with sugar and cinnamon and serve with a fruit sauce.

ALMOND CIRCLES

INGREDIENTS	Metric	Imperial	American
Flour	500 g	1 lb 2 oz	$4\frac{1}{2}$ cups
Yeast	40 g	$1\frac{1}{2}$ oz	$1\frac{1}{2}$ oz
Sugar	50 g	2 oz	$\frac{1}{4}$ cup
Milk	125 ml	4 fl oz	$\frac{1}{2}$ cup
Salt	$\frac{1}{2}$ tsp	$\frac{1}{2}$ tsp	$\frac{1}{2}$ tsp
Eggs	2	2	2
Almonds	40 g	$1\frac{1}{2}$ oz	$\frac{1}{3}$ cup
Oil	8 tbsp	8 tbsp	8 tbsp
Coarse sugar, for dusting			

1. Combine the ingredients to make a yeast dough, including the chopped almonds. Roll out the dough 5 mm $\frac{1}{4}$ thick and cut out rounds with 7 cm/$2\frac{3}{4}$ in diameter. Out of each centre, cut a circle of 2 cm /$\frac{3}{4}$ in diameter to make rings. Leave to rise a little, then deep-fry in the hot oil. Drain, then turn in the sugar.

Cooking time: 4-5 minutes

BUTTER KNOTS

INGREDIENTS	Metric	Imperial	American
Butter	150 g	5 oz	$\frac{2}{3}$ cup
Sugar	150 g	5 oz	$\frac{2}{3}$ cup
Eggs	3	3	3
Single cream	$\frac{1}{2}$ tbsp	$\frac{1}{2}$ tbsp	$\frac{1}{2}$ tbsp
Rum	$\frac{1}{2}$ tbsp	$\frac{1}{2}$ tbsp	$\frac{1}{2}$ tbsp
Lemon rind, grated			
Flour	600 g	$1\frac{1}{2}$ lb	6 cups
Baking powder	2 tsp	2 tsp	2 tsp
Icing sugar			

1. Combine all the ingredients to make a smooth shortcrust pastry. Roll out, then cut out rectangles 15 cm/6 in long and 2 cm/$\frac{3}{4}$ in wide. Tie the strips into knots and bake in the hot fat. Drain, then dust with icing sugar.

Cooking time: 4-5 minutes

GOLD BALLS

INGREDIENTS	Metric	Imperial	American
Butter	100 g	4 oz	$\frac{1}{2}$ cup
Water	250 ml	9 fl oz	1 cup + 2 tbsp
Salt	1 pinch	1 pinch	1 pinch
Sugar	1 tbsp	1 tbsp	1 tbsp
Flour	150 g	$5\frac{1}{2}$ oz	$1\frac{1}{2}$ cups
Eggs	6	6	6
Icing sugar			

1. Bring the butter, water, salt and sugar to the boil, then pour in the flour in one go and stir vigorously until the dough comes off the base of the pan. Remove the pan from the heat and stir in the eggs, one at a time. Using a teaspoon, take walnut-size balls from the pastry and drop into the hot oil, using a second teaspoon. After 3 minutes, turn the balls. Drain, then dust with icing sugar.

Cooking time: 4 minutes

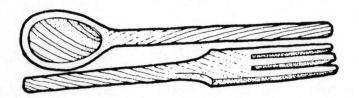

PASTRY SHAVINGS

INGREDIENTS	Metric	Imperial	American
Margarine	150 g	5 oz	$\frac{2}{3}$ cup
Sugar	75 g	3 oz	$\frac{1}{3}$ cup
Vanilla essence	a few drops	a few drops	a few drops
Lemon, grated rind	1	1	1
Eggs	2	2	2
Cornflour	125 g	$4\frac{1}{2}$ oz	$4\frac{1}{4}$ cups
Flour	375 g	13 oz	$3\frac{1}{4}$ cups
Baking powder	3 tsp	3 tsp	3 tsp
Milk	4 tbsp	4 tbsp	4 tbsp
Icing sugar for dusting			

1. Whisk the margarine, sugar, vanilla essence, lemon rind and the eggs until creamy. Combine the cornflour, flour and baking powder and add to the mixture with the milk. Then knead the dough and roll out 5 mm/$\frac{1}{4}$ thick. Cut out diamond shapes, make a cut in the centre and pull one end of the diamond through the cut. Bake the 'shavings' in the hot oil. Drain, then dust with icing sugar.

Cooking time: 5 minutes

FRENCH CRUELLERS

INGREDIENTS	Metric	Imperial	American
Water	500 ml	18 fl oz	$2\frac{1}{4}$ cups
Margarine	125 g	$4\frac{1}{2}$ oz	$\frac{2}{3}$ cup
Salt	1 pinch	1 pinch	1 pinch
Sugar	1 tbsp	1 tbsp	1 tbsp
Flour	250 g	9 oz	$2\frac{1}{4}$ cups
Eggs	4	4	4
For the icing:			
Icing sugar	250 g	9 oz	1 cup
Juice of lemon	$\frac{1}{2}$	$\frac{1}{2}$	$\frac{1}{2}$
Water	a little	a little	a little

1. Make a pastry out of the top ingredients, as described for the goldballs. Transfer the pastry into a piping bag and pipe a small circle on to a strip of greaseproof paper that has been dipped into the hot oil. Dip each circle with the paper into the hot oil and let it glide off. Turning occasionally, bake until the ring is golden brown on both sides.

Cooking time: 5 minutes

2. After draining, cover with thick icing made by combining the icing sugar, lemon juice and a little water.

DOUGHNUTS WITH DATES

INGREDIENTS	Metric	Imperial	American
Dates	25 g	1 oz	1 oz
Cherry brandy	1 tbsp	1 tbsp	1 tbsp
Almonds	25 g	1 oz	$\frac{1}{4}$ cup
Water	250 ml	9 fl oz	1 cup + 2 tbsp
Margarine	60 g	$2\frac{1}{2}$ oz	$\frac{1}{4}$ cup
Salt	1 pinch	1 pinch	1 pinch
Flour			
Eggs	4	4	4
Icing sugar			

1. Stone the dates, sprinkle with cherry brandy and fill with a peeled almond each. Bring the water with the margarine and the salt to the boil, then pour in all the flour in one go and stir over the heat constantly, until the dough easily comes off the base of the pan. Immediately stir in 1 egg, leave the dough to cool, then stir in the remaining eggs.

2. Coat each date singly with the dough, deep-fry in the hot oil, drain and sprinkle with icing sugar. Serve warm or cold.

Cooking time: 4 minutes

BERLIN DOUGHNUTS

INGREDIENTS	Metric	Imperial	American
Flour	500 g	1 lb 2 oz	$4\frac{1}{2}$ cups
Yeast	40 g	$1\frac{1}{2}$ oz	$1\frac{1}{2}$ oz
Milk	125 ml	4 fl oz	$\frac{1}{2}$ cup
Sugar	100 g	4 oz	$\frac{1}{2}$ cup
Salt			
Margarine	40 g	$1\frac{1}{2}$ oz	3 tbsp
Lemon rind, grated			
Egg (reserve some egg white)	1	1	1
Preserve for filling			
Sugar for coating			

1. Prepare a yeast dough from the flour, yeast, milk, sugar, salt, margarine, lemon rind and egg and roll out 5 mm/$\frac{1}{4}$ in thick. Using a glass, mark circles on half the dough, place a little preserve in the centre, and brush the edges with egg white. Fold over the other half of the dough and cut out the circles, making sure the preserve is right in the centre. Firmly press the edges together.

2. Leave the doughnuts to rise again, then bake in the hot oil until golden brown. Turn in sugar.

Cooking time: 4 minutes

9. SAUCES

Cold sauces

PIQUANT SAUCE

INGREDIENTS	Metric	Imperial	American
Hard-boiled egg yolks	4	4	4
Red wine	4 tbsp	4 tbsp	4 tbsp
Oil	4 tbsp	4 tbsp	4 tbsp
Mustard	1 tbsp	1 tbsp	1 tbsp
Lemon juice	1	1	1
Sugar	1 pinch	1 pinch	1 pinch
Salt			
Pepper			

1. Press the egg yolks through a fine sieve, then combine with the wine and the oil. Add mustard, lemon juice, sugar and seasoning to taste.

DEVIL'S SAUCE

INGREDIENTS	Metric	Imperial	American
Oil	3 tbsp	3 tbsp	3 tbsp
Tomato ketchup	4 tbsp	4 tbsp	4 tbsp
Onion	1	1	1
Olives	75 g	3 oz	$\frac{1}{2}$ cup
Brandy	2 tsp	2 tsp	2 tsp
Parsley			
Dillweed			
Salt			
Cayenne pepper			

1. Whisk the oil with the ketchup. Add the onion, finely diced, and finely sliced olives, then the brandy, and some herbs and seasoning. This sauce goes well with fried and deep-fried meat.

CALIFORNIAN SAUCE

INGREDIENTS	Metric	Imperial	American
Tomato ketchup	1 tbsp	1 tbsp	1 tbsp
Evaporated milk	4 tbsp	4 tbsp	4 tbsp
Oil	1 tbsp	2 tbsp	2 tbsp
Lemon juice			
Salt			
Pepper			
Sugar			
Worcestershire sauce			

1. Combine the ketchup with the milk and oil and add the remaining ingredients to taste.

ORANGE SAUCE

INGREDIENTS	Metric	Imperial	American
Lemon juice	2	2	2
Orance juice	2	2	2
Sugar	100 g	4 oz	$\frac{1}{2}$ cup
Slice of bread, thick	1	1	1
White wine	125 ml	4 fl oz	$\frac{1}{2}$ cup
Horseradish, grated	100 g	4 oz	4 oz
Single cream	75 ml	3 fl oz	6 tbsp
Egg yolks, hard boiled	3	3	3
Lemon juice			
Worcestershire sauce			
Salt	1 pinch	1 pinch	1 pinch
Pepper			

1. Bring the lemon and orange juice and the sugar to the boil, then leave to cool.

2. Soak the bread in wine and squeeze dry, then combine with the horseradish, cream and egg yolks. Whisk in the juices and add the remaining ingredients and seasoning to taste.

SWEDISH SAUCE

INGREDIENTS	Metric	Imperial	American
Mayonnaise	2 tbsp	2 tbsp	2 tbsp
Apple purée	1 tbsp	1 tbsp	1 tbsp
Grated horseradish	1 tsp	1 tsp	1 tsp
Lemon juice			
Salt			
Pepper			

1. Combine the mayonnaise with the remaining ingredients, seasoning to taste.

SAUCE VERTE

INGREDIENTS	Metric	Imperial	American
Soured cream	250 ml	9 fl oz	1 cup + 2 tbsp
Milk	1-2 tbsp	1-2 tbsp	1-2 tbsp
Lemon juice	$\frac{1}{2}$	$\frac{1}{2}$	$\frac{1}{2}$
Mustard	1 tbsp	1 tbsp	1 tbsp
Salt			
Pepper			
Eggs, hard boiled	2	2	2
Pickled cucumber	1	1	1
Onion	1	1	1
Fresh herbs, chopped	2 tbsp	2 tbsp	2 tbsp

1. Whisk the cream with the milk and the lemon juice, then season with mustard, salt and pepper. Finely dice the eggs, cucumber and onion and add to the cream with the herbs. Serve well chilled.

Warm sauces

MINCE SAUCE

INGREDIENTS	Metric	Imperial	American
Streaky smoked bacon	50 g	2 oz	2 oz
Onion	1	1	1
Minced beef	200 g	7 oz	1 cup
Tomatoes, peeled and diced	3	3	3
Water	250 ml	9 fl oz	1 cup + 2 tbsp
Gravy granules	2 tbsp	2 tbsp	2 tbsp
Cream			
Pepper			

1. Dice the bacon and the onion and gently fry in a pan, then add the mince and tomatoes. Add the water, then leave to simmer for 5 minutes. Stir in the gravy granules and add cream and pepper to taste.

HORSERADISH SAUCE

INGREDIENTS	Metric	Imperial	American
Onion	1 small	1 small	1 small
Fat	30 g	1 oz	2 tbsp
Flour	30 g	1 oz	$\frac{1}{3}$ cup
Water	250 ml	9 fl oz	1 cup + 2 tbsp
Milk	250 ml	9 fl oz	1 cup + 2 tbsp
Mayonnaise	50 g	2 oz	2 oz
Grated horseradish, to taste			
Salt			
Sugar			

1. Gently fry the finely chopped onion in the fat. Dust in the flour, simmer a little and pour in the water. Add the milk and leave to boil. Remove from the heat and add the mayonnaise, and the horseradish, sugar and salt to taste. To quicken the process, you can use a ready-mix white sauce.

HAM-CHASSEUR SAUCE

INGREDIENTS	Metric	Imperial	American
Onion	1	1	1
Ham	3 slices	3 slices	3 slices
Oil	2 tbsp	2 tbsp	2 tbsp
Tomato purée	1 tbsp	1 tbsp	1 tbsp
Water	250 ml	9 fl oz	1 cup + 2 tbsp
Chasseur seasoning mix	1 packet	1 packet	1 packet
Evaporated milk	2 tbsp	2 tbsp	2 tbsp
Lemon juice			
Sugar			

1. Gently fry the chopped onion and ham in the hot oil, adding the tomato purée. Pour in the water and then stir in the seasoning mix, according to the instructions on the packet. Let it simmer for about 6 minutes. Then add the milk and the lemon juice and sugar to taste.

CAPER SAUCE

INGREDIENTS	Metric	Imperial	American
Margarine	30 g	1 oz	2 tbsp
Flour	30 g	1 oz	$\frac{1}{3}$ cup
Stock	250 ml	9 fl oz	1 cup + 2 tbsp
Milk	250 ml	9 fl oz	1 cup + 2 tbsp
Egg yolk, or	1	1	1
mayonnaise	2 tbsp	2 tbsp	2 tbsp
Capers	2 tbsp	2 tbsp	2 tbsp
Salt			
Sugar			
Lemon juice			

1. Prepare a white sauce from the margarine, flour and the stock. Add the milk and leave to simmer for 10 minutes. Bind the sauce with an egg yolk or mayonnaise, then add the capers and salt, sugar and lemon juice to taste.

POLISH SAUCE

INGREDIENTS	Metric	Imperial	American
Red wine	125 ml	4 fl oz	$\frac{1}{2}$ cup
Water	125 ml	4 fl oz	$\frac{1}{2}$ cup
Instant beef sauce mix	1 packet	1 packet	1 packet
Raisins	1 tbsp	1 tbsp	1 tbsp
Almonds	1 tbsp	1 tbsp	1 tbsp
Cinnamon	1 pinch	1 pinch	1 pinch
Clove	1	1	1
Lemon rind, grated			

1. Prepare the instant sauce according to the instructions on the packet, using the red wine and water as the liquid. Add the raisins and almonds and add cinnamon, cloves and lemon rind to taste. Serve this sauce with boiled eel and a chicory salad.

PAPRIKA CREAM SAUCE

INGREDIENTS	Metric	Imperial	American
Onion	1 large	1 large	1 large
Margarine	20 g	$\frac{3}{4}$ oz	1 tbsp
Flour	20 g	$\frac{3}{4}$ oz	$\frac{1}{3}$ cup
Paprika purée	1 tbsp	1 tbsp	1 tbsp
Stock, from cube	250 ml	9 fl oz	1 cup + 2 tbsp
Red pepper	1	1	1
Salt			
Cayenne pepper			
Paprika			
Sugar, to taste			
Whipping cream	125 ml	4 fl oz	$\frac{1}{2}$ cup

1. Gently fry the diced onion in the margarine and sauté the flour until light yellow. Add the paprika purée, then pour in the stock. Add the diced pepper and leave to simmer for approximately 15 minutes. Add a little sugar and season to taste. Remove the pan from the heat and fold in the whipped cream.

SAVOURY SAUCE

INGREDIENTS	Metric	Imperial	American
Ham, finely diced	50 g	2 oz	$\frac{1}{4}$ cup
Onion, chopped	1	1	1
Oil	2 tbsp	2 tbsp	2 tbsp
Tomatoes, diced	2	2	2
Water	250 ml	9 fl oz	1 cup + 2 tbsp
Instant beef sauce mix	1 packet	1 packet	1 packet
Horseradish, grated			
Parsley, finely chopped			

1. Sauté the ham and onion in the hot oil. Add the tomatoes and simmer. Pour in the prepared sauce mix, bring to boil, stirring, and leave to simmer for 1 minute over low heat. Add horseradish and parsley to taste.

HOT TOMATO SAUCE

INGREDIENTS	Metric	Imperial	American
Tomato sauce mix	1 packet	1 packet	1 packet
Water	250 ml	9 fl oz	1 cup + 2 tbsp
Single cream or evaporated milk	2 tbsp	2 tbsp	2 tbsp
Anchovy fillets	5	5	5
Onion	1	1	1
Parsley	1 bunch	1 bunch	1 bunch
Chives	1 bunch	1 bunch	1 bunch
Salt			
Pepper			
Paprika			

1. Prepare the tomato sauce according to the instructions on the packet, using the water and the cream. Add the finely chopped anchovies, onion, parsley and chives. Season to taste with salt, pepper and paprika.

MUSTARD SAUCE WITH CAPERS

INGREDIENTS	Metric	Imperial	American
Margarine	40 g	1½ oz	3 tbsp
Flour	40 g	1½ oz	⅓ cup
Stock, from cube	500 ml	18 fl oz	2¼ cups
Mustard	1 tbsp	1 tbsp	1 tbsp
Capers	1 tbsp	1 tbsp	1 tbsp
Salt			

1. Prepare a white sauce and add the mustard, capers and a little salt for seasoning salt. To enhance the flavour, you can add a dash of white wine or a few drops of lemon juice.

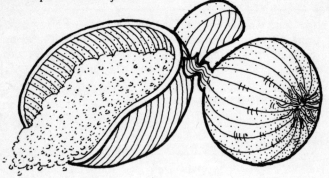

CHEESE SAUCE

INGREDIENTS	Metric	Imperial	American
Ready-mix savoury white sauce	1 packet	1 packet	1 packet
Water	250 ml	9 fl oz	1 cup + 2 tbsp
Cheese spread	1 triangle	1 triangle	1 triangle
Salt			
Fresh chilli, finely chopped	1	1	1
Garlic clove, finely chopped	1	1	1
Egg yolk	1	1	1

1. Prepare the white sauce according to the instructions on the packet. Add the cheese and stir until it has dissolved. Add salt, chilli and garlic, then bind with the egg yolk.

SHERRY SAUCE

INGREDIENTS	Metric	Imperial	American
Onion	1 small	1 small	1 small
Margarine	30 g	1 oz	2 tbsp
Flour	20 g	$\frac{3}{4}$ oz	$\frac{1}{3}$ cup
Sherry	$\frac{1}{2}$ cup	$\frac{1}{2}$ cup	$\frac{1}{2}$ cup
Tomato ketchup	2 tbsp	2 tbsp	2 tbsp
Lemon juice	1 tbsp	1 tbsp	1 tbsp
Sugar	a little	a little	a little
Salt			

1. Gently fry the diced onion in the margarine, then sprinkle over the flour and sauté a little. Add sherry, ketchup, lemon juice and sugar. Bring to the boil once, then season to taste. Serve with mince meat dishes.

CURRY SAUCE

INGREDIENTS	Metric	Imperial	American
Ready-mix white sauce	1 packet	1 packet	1 packet
Water	500 ml	18 fl oz	$2\frac{1}{4}$ cups
Red pepper	1 small	1 small	1 small
Green pepper	1 small	1 small	1 small
Salt			
Curry	$1\frac{1}{2}$ tsp	$1\frac{1}{2}$ tsp	$1\frac{1}{2}$ tsp
Single cream or evaporated milk	2-3 tbsp	2-3 tbsp	2-3 tbsp

1. Prepare the white sauce according to the instructions on the packet, using the water. Slice the peppers very finely and add to the sauce, with some salt. Leave to simmer for 10 minutes. Before serving, add the curry and the cream.

Sweet Sauces for Sweets

WINE CREAM SAUCE

INGREDIENTS	Metric	Imperial	American
Eggs	2	2	2
Sugar	50 g	2 oz	$\frac{1}{4}$ cup
Cornflour	2 tsp	2 tsp	2 tsp
White wine	250 ml	9 fl oz	1 cup + 2 tbsp
Lemon rind, grated			
Lemon juice	2 tbsp	2 tbsp	2 tbsp

1. Combine all ingredients in a high pan over low heat with an electric mixer until the mixture starts rising and thickening. Serve warm or cold.

APRICOT SAUCE

INGREDIENTS	Metric	Imperial	American
Apricots, can	1 small	1 small	1 small
Whipping cream	125 ml	4 fl oz	$\frac{1}{2}$ cup
Sugar	1 heaped tbsp	1 heaped tbsp	1 heaped tbsp
Apricot brandy	2 tbsp	2 tbsp	2 tbsp

1. Drain the apricots well, then purée in a food processor. Add the cream and sugar and continue whipping until the cream turns thick. Then add the brandy.

FRUIT SAUCE

INGREDIENTS	Metric	Imperial	American
Berries, according to season	250 g	9 oz	$1\frac{1}{2}$ cups
Water	500 ml	18 fl oz	$2\frac{1}{4}$ cups
Cornflour	$\frac{1}{2}$ tsp	$\frac{1}{2}$ tsp	$\frac{1}{2}$ tsp
Sugar, to taste			
Lemon juice	a few drops	a few drops	a few drops

1. Wash and clean the berries, then bring to boil in the water. Press through a fine sieve, then thicken the fruit juice with the cornflour. Add sugar and lemon juice to taste.

ORANGE SAUCE

INGREDIENTS	Metric	Imperial	American
Sugar	80 g	3 oz	$\frac{1}{3}$ cup
Orange juice	125 ml	4 fl oz	$\frac{1}{2}$ cup
Lemon rind, grated	$\frac{1}{2}$	$\frac{1}{2}$	$\frac{1}{2}$
Lemon, finely cut rind	$\frac{1}{2}$	$\frac{1}{2}$	$\frac{1}{2}$
Lemon juice	4 tbsp	4 tbsp	4 tbsp
Cointreau	6 tbsp	6 tbsp	6 tbsp

1. Caramelise the sugar. Add the orange juice and the lemon rind and juice, and reduce by boiling to a third. Finally, add the Cointreau and serve with freshly deep-fried cakes.

DRIED FRUIT SAUCE

INGREDIENTS	Metric	Imperial	American
Onion	1	1	1
Fat	20 g	$\frac{3}{4}$ oz	1 heaped tbsp
Dried apricots	125 g	$4\frac{1}{2}$ oz	1 cup
Prunes, stoned	125 g	$4\frac{1}{2}$ oz	1 cup
Water	500 ml	18 fl oz	$2\frac{1}{4}$ cups
Red wine	250 ml	9 fl oz	1 cup + 2 tbsp
Sugar	2 tbsp	2 tbsp	2 tbsp
Cornflour, for binding			
Flaked almonds	1 packet	1 packet	1 packet

1. Gently fry the diced onion in the fat, then add the apricots and prunes and pour in the water and wine and add the sugar. Leave to simmer for 20 minutes over low heat, then bind with the cornflour. Sprinkle with flaked almonds and serve.

RED WINE SAUCE

INGREDIENTS	Metric	Imperial	American
Light red wine	500 ml	18 fl oz	$2\frac{1}{4}$ cups
Cloves	2	2	2
Cinnamon stick	a piece	a piece	a piece
Grated orange rind			
Sugar	50 g	2 oz	$\frac{1}{4}$ cup
Lemon juice	1 tbsp	1 tbsp	1 tbsp
Cornflour	1 tbsp	1 tbsp	1 tbsp

1. Bring the wine with the cloves, cinnamon, orange rind, sugar and lemon juice to the boil, then bind with the cornflour. Pour through a fine sieve and serve with deep-fried desserts.

CARAMEL SAUCE

INGREDIENTS	Metric	Imperial	American
Sugar	100 g	4 oz	$\frac{1}{2}$ cup
Water	125 ml	4 fl oz	$\frac{1}{2}$ cup
Milk	500 ml	18 fl oz	$2\frac{1}{4}$ cups
Vanilla pod	$\frac{1}{2}$	$\frac{1}{2}$	$\frac{1}{2}$
Cornflour	2 tbsp	2 tbsp	2 tbsp
Egg yolk	1	1	1

1. Gently brown the sugar in an open pan, then pour in boiling water. As soon as the sugar has dissolved, add the hot milk, reserving 2 tbsp cold milk. Halve the vanilla pod lengthways, scrape out the marrow and add to the sauce. Combine the cornflour with the reserved milk and the egg yolk, stir into the sauce and briefly bring to the boil again.

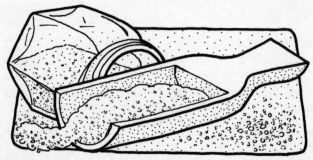

BLUEBERRY SAUCE

INGREDIENTS	Metric	Imperial	American
Blueberries	2 tbsp	2 tbsp	2 tbsp
Water	375 ml	13 fl oz	1¾ cups
Sugar			
Cornflour	2 tbsp	2 tbsp	2 tbsp
Red wine	125 ml	4 fl oz	½ cup

1. Bring the berries to the boil with the water, sweeten to taste, and bind with the cornflour. Add the red wine. This sauce goes very well with sweet doughnuts and gold balls.

FLUFFY ORANGE SAUCE

INGREDIENTS	Metric	Imperial	American
White wine	125 ml	4 fl oz	½ cup
Oranges, juice	2	2	2
Lemon, juice	1	1	1
Orange, grated rind	½	½	½
Sugar	50 g	2 oz	¼ cup
Eggs	2	2	2
Cornflour	2 tsp	2 tsp	2 tsp
Rum	a dash	a dash	a dash

1. Combine the wine with the orange and lemon juice, orange rind, sugar, eggs and cornflour in a high pan and whisk vigorously over low heat until the sauce just begins to boil. Immediately remove from the heat and add the rum.

10. SALADS TO COMPLEMENT A DEEP-FRIED MEAL

FRUIT SALAD WITH CREAM

INGREDIENTS	Metric	Imperial	American
Peach halves	2	2	2
Pear halves	2	2	2
Pineapple	1 slice	1 slice	1 slice
Cream, whipped	125 ml	4 fl oz	$\frac{1}{2}$ cup
Cherry brandy	3-4 tbsp	3-4 tbsp	3-4 tbsp
Sugar	40 g	1$\frac{1}{2}$ oz	3 tbsp
Cocktail cherries			

1. Cut the peach and pear in two and the pineapple into 6 pieces. Combine the cream with the cherry brandy and the sugar and sprinkle over the salad. Decorate with cherries.

DIPLOMAT SALAD

INGREDIENTS	Metric	Imperial	American
Pineapple, diced	200 g	7 oz	7 oz
Celery sticks, diced	100 g	4 oz	4 oz
Walnuts, chopped	100 g	4 oz	1 cup
Mayonnaise			
Tomatoes	4 large	4 large	4 large
Lettuce			

1. Combine the pineapple with the celery and the walnuts, then stir in the mayonnaise. Fill this mixture into the scooped out tomatoes and arrange on lettuce leaves.

76

RED CABBAGE SALAD

INGREDIENTS	Metric	Imperial	American
Red cabbage	300 g	11 oz	11 oz
Apples	4	4	4
Oil	5 tbsp	5 tbsp	5 tbsp
Vinegar	3 tbsp	3 tbsp	3 tbsp
Honey	1 tbsp	1 tbsp	1 tbsp
Ground cloves			
Salt			
Sugar			

1. Quarter the cabbage, then shred very finely. Peel the apples if necessary, grate them coarsely and mix with the cabbage. Combine the remaining ingredients to make a dressing, pour over the salad and leave to marinate for a few hours.

RAW CAULIFLOWER PLATTER

INGREDIENTS	Metric	Imperial	American
Cauliflower	1	1	1
Carrots	250 g	9 oz	2 medium
Green peas, frozen	125 g	$4\frac{1}{2}$ oz	2 cups
Single cream	250 ml	9 fl oz	1 cup 2 tbsp
Lemon juice	2 tbsp	2 tbsp	2 tbsp
Mayonnaise	1 tbsp	1 tbsp	1 tbsp
Nutmeg			
Salad seasoning			
Salt			
Sugar			
Herbs, chopped			

1. Wash and separate the cauliflower, clean the carrots and then grate both coarsely. Thaw the peas.

2. Beat the cream with the lemon juice, mayonnaise, nutmeg, seasoning and a little sugar and fold under the vegetables. Sprinkle with herbs and serve.

MIXED VEGETABLE SALAD

INGREDIENTS	Metric	Imperial	American
Potatoes, boiled	4	4	4
Young green beans	1 cup	1 cup	1 cup
Young peas	1 cup	1 cup	1 cup
Eggs, hard boiled	2	2	2
Onion	1 large	1 large	1 large
Marinated red pepper	1	1	1
Soured cream	1 carton	1 carton	1 carton
Wine vinegar			
Oil			
Salt			
Pepper			
Estragon			
Pimpinella			
Lettuce hearts	2	2	2

1. Dice the potatoes. Combine them with the beans, peas, sliced eggs, sliced onion, and cut pepper. Combine the cream, vinegar, oil, seasoning and herbs to make a dressing, and pour it over the salad. Before serving, add the shredded lettuce.

AMERICAN SALAD

INGREDIENTS	Metric	Imperial	American
Lettuce	1 large	1 large	1 large
Orange	1	1	1
Pineapple, slices	2	2	2
Orange juice	1 tbsp	1 tbsp	1 tbsp
Lemon juice	1 tbsp	1 tbsp	1 tbsp
Salt			
Pepper			
Sugar	1 pinch	1 pinch	1 pinch
Oil	2-3 tbsp	2-3 tbsp	2-3 tbsp

1. Wash the salad, tearing the larger leaves. Peel and dice the orange, dice the pineapple. Make a dressing from the remaining ingredients, pour over the salad, toss and serve.

SERBIAN SALAD

INGREDIENTS	Metric	Imperial	American
Green peppers	200 g	7 oz	7 oz
Red peppers	200 g	7 oz	7 oz
Apples	200 g	7 oz	7 oz
Celeriac	125 g	$4\frac{1}{2}$ oz	$4\frac{1}{2}$ oz
Oil	5 tbsp	5 tbsp	5 tbsp
Vinegar	2 tbsp	2 tbsp	2 tbsp
Onion	1	1	1
Salt			
Sugar			

1. Seed and wash the peppers, then cut them into strips. Grate the apples and the cleaned celeriac. Combine the remaining ingredients to make a dressing, pour over the salad, toss and leave to marinate.

EXQUISITE POTATO SALAD

INGREDIENTS	Metric	Imperial	American
Potatoes, boiled	750 g	$1\frac{1}{2}$ lb	$1\frac{1}{2}$ lb
Oranges	2	2	2
Celery hearts, tinned	225 g	8 oz	8 oz
Mayonnaise	100 g	4 oz	4 oz
Salt			
Pepper			
Lemon juice			
Sugar	1 pinch	1 pinch	1 pinch

1. Peel the potatoes and the oranges and cut into strips; cut the celery into strips. Combine the mayonnaise with the rest of the ingredients, spoon over the potato-orange-celery mixture and leave to marinate. Serve well chilled.

ARTICHOKE SALAD

INGREDIENTS	Metric	Imperial	American
Artichokes, canned	8-10	8-10	8-10
Oranges	2	2	2
Salt			
Sugar			
Wine vinegar	2 tbsp	2 tbsp	2 tbsp
Chopped parsley	1 tbsp	1 tbsp	1 tbsp
Chopped chives	1 tbsp	1 tbsp	1 tbsp
Boiled eggs	2	2	2
Onion	1 large	1 large	1 large
Brandy	1 small glass	1 small glass	1 small glass
Flaked almonds	1 tbsp	1 tbsp	1 tbsp
Remoulade sauce	3 tbsp	3 tbsp	3 tbsp

1. Drain the artichoke hearts, then cut into strips. Finely cut the oranges. Reserve the juice and add the orange pieces to the artichokes. Combine the orange juice with salt, sugar and vinegar, then add the herbs and the chopped eggs and pour this marinade over the salad. Leave to marinate for 1 hour.

2. Combine the very finely chopped onion with the brandy, almonds and the remoulade, pour over the salad and serve immediately.

SPICY PEA SALAD

INGREDIENTS	Metric	Imperial	American
Green peas, frozen	300 g	11 oz	5 cups
Apple, slightly sour	1	1	1
Banana	1	1	1
Mortadella sausage	150 g	5 oz	5 oz
Mushrooms, can	$\frac{L}{3}$	$\frac{L}{3}$	$\frac{L}{3}$
Chopped parsley			
Water	250ml	9 fl oz	1 cup + 2 tbsp
Ready-made tomato sauce	1 packet	1 packet	1 packet

	Metric	Imperial	American
Mayonnaise	100 g	4 oz	4 oz
Lemon juice	2 tbsp	2 tbsp	2 tbsp
Tomato ketchup	1 tbsp	1 tbsp	2 tbsp
Liquid paprika	1 tbsp	1 tbsp	1 tbsp

1. Defrost the peas. Dice the apple, banana and the mortadella, then add the mushrooms and parsley.

2. Prepare the tomato sauce according to the instructions on the packet, then stir in the mayonnaise. Add lemon juice, ketchup and paprika to taste. Pour over the salad, mix well and leave to marinate.

KOHLRABI SALAD

INGREDIENTS	Metric	Imperial	American
Kohlrabi	3	3	3
Radishes	2 bunches	2 bunches	2 bunches
Lemon juice	2 tbsp	2 tbsp	2 tbsp
Water	2 tbsp	2 tbsp	2 tbsp
Sugar	1 tbsp	1 tbsp	1 tbsp
Salt			
Pepper			
Oil	1 tbsp	1 tbsp	1 tbsp
Yoghurt	1 carton	1 carton	1 carton
Mayonnaise	2 tbsp	2 tbsp	2 tbsp
Evaporated milk	2 tbsp	2 tbsp	2 tbsp
Sugar			
Paprika			
Mustard			
Cress	50 g	2 oz	2 oz

1. Peel the kohlrabi, then cut into matchstick-size pieces. Wash and slice the radishes. Combine the lemon juice with the water, sugar, salt, pepper, and oil and pour over the salad and mix. Arrange on a platter.

2. Whisk the yoghurt with the mayonnaise, milk, sugar, salt, paprika and mustard and pour over the centre of the salad. Garnish with the cress.

SWISS SALAD

INGREDIENTS	Metric	Imperial	American
Potatoes	750 g	1½ lb	1½ lb
Oil	2 tbsp	2 tbsp	2 tbsp
Celery salt			
Garlic salt			
Onion salt			
Pepper			
Cheese, mixed	250 g	9 oz	9 oz
Apple	1	1	1
Lemon juice			
Cornichons	3	3	3
Onions	2 small	2 small	2 small
Tomatoes	2	2	2
Green peppers	2	2	2
Ham	100 g	4 oz	4 oz
Parsley			
Dillweed			
Chives			
Chervil			
Cream	125 ml	4 fl oz	½ cup
Yoghurt	1 carton	1 carton	1 carton
Mustard	1 tbsp	1 tbsp	1 tbsp
Processed cheese, slices	3	3	3
Vinegar	2 tbsp	2 tbsp	2 tbsp
Salt			
Sugar			
Salad seasoning			
Lettuce leaves			
Radishes			

1. Peel the boiled, chilled potatoes and dice them. Sprinkle with oil, season to taste and mix carefully. Coarsely grate the cheese, the peeled apple, sprinkled with lemon juice, and the cornichons. Finely chop the

onions, dice the tomatoes. Wash and seed, then finely cut the peppers. Finely chop the ham and the herbs. Mix everything carefully with the potatoes.

2. Combine all but last two remaining ingredients to make a dressing and fold into the salad.

3. Cover a deep plate with lettuce leaves, arrange the salad on them and decorate with the radishes.

ASPARAGUS EGG SALAD

INGREDIENTS	Metric	Imperial	American
Fresh, cooked asparagus, or:	500 g	1 lb	1 lb
asparagus tips, can	1	1	1
Eggs, hard-boiled	3	3	3
Cornichon	1	1	1
Dillweed			
Chervil			
Parsley			
Oil	4 tbsp	4 tbsp	4 tbsp
Vinegar	2 tbsp	2 tbsp	2 tbsp
Evaporated milk	1 tbsp	1 tbsp	1 tbsp
Salt			
Sugar			
Pepper			
Paprika			
Liquid garlic			

1. Drain the asparagus. Cut the eggs into wedges, thinly slice the cornichon. Finely chop the herbs and carefully mix these ingredients. Combine the remaining ingredients to make a dressing, pour over the salad and mix well. Serve immediately.

BEAN SALAD WITH SALAMI

INGREDIENTS	Metric	Imperial	American
Oil	4 tbsp	4 tbsp	4 tbsp
Vinegar	2 tbsp	2 tbsp	2 tbsp
Mustard	1 tsp	1 tsp	1 tsp
Onion	1	1	1
Salt			
Tabasco sauce	2 dashes	2 dashes	2 dashes
Haricot beans, can	1 large	1 large	1 large
Salami	200 g	7 oz	7 oz

1. Combine the oil, vinegar and the mustard. Peel and finely chop the onion and add to the dressing. Season with salt and tabasco. Drain the beans, dice the salami and transfer to the dressing. Leave to marinate for 1 hour.

ANDALUSIAN SALAD

INGREDIENTS	Metric	Imperial	American
Rice	100 g	4 oz	$\frac{1}{2}$ cup
Salted water			
Oil	3 tbsp	3 tbsp	3 tbsp
Vinegar	3 tbsp	3 tbsp	3 tbsp
Salt			
Paprika			
Mushrooms, sautéed	125 g	$4\frac{1}{2}$ oz	$4\frac{1}{2}$ oz
Olives	2 tbsp	2 tbsp	2 tbsp
Ham	100 g	4 oz	4 oz
Green pepper	1	1	1
Chopped parsley	1 tbsp	1 tbsp	1 tbsp

1. Boil the rice in plenty of salted water, then rinse with cold water and leave to drain. Then combine with a dressing made from oil, vinegar, salt and paprika. Add the remaining ingredients diced or sliced, and mix well. Sprinkle with the parsley and leave to marinate.

RAW SALAD WITH CARROTS, PINEAPPLE, AND CHICORY

INGREDIENTS	Metric	Imperial	American
Carrots	250 g	9 oz	2 medium
Chicory, heads	3	3	3
Pineapple, slices	3	3	3
Yoghurt	1 carton	1 carton	1 carton
Oil	2 tbsp	2 tbsp	2 tbsp
Lemon, juice	1	1	1
Salt			
Sugar			

1. Clean the carrots and grate finely. Trim the chicory, cut it in half and discard the bitter centre. Slice thinly and immediately sprinkle with lemon juice. Cut the pineapple into small pieces. Mix the carrots, chicory and pineapple.

2. For the dressing, the yoghurt with the oil and lemon juice, add sugar and seasoning to taste and pour over the salad shortly before serving.

RICE SALAD WITH HAM

INGREDIENTS	Metric	Imperial	American
Boiled rice	3 cups	3 cups	3 cups
Remoulade sauce	1 cup	1 cup	1 cup
Lean smoked ham	200 g	7 oz	7 oz
Chopped chives	1 tbsp	1 tbsp	1 tbsp
Tomatoes	2	2	2
Red wine	$\frac{1}{2}$ cup	$\frac{1}{2}$ cup	$\frac{1}{2}$ cup
Almond pieces	$\frac{1}{2}$ cup	$\frac{1}{2}$ cup	$\frac{1}{2}$ cup
Salt			
Pepper			

1. Combine the rice with the remoulade and mix in the ham, cut into strips. Leave to marinate for 20 minutes. Add the chives, the peeled and diced tomatoes, wine and almonds. Season to taste with salt and pepper.

CHANTERELLE SALAD WITH CORNICHONS AND RICE

INGREDIENTS	Metric	Imperial	American
Chanterelles, can	1 small	1 small	1 small
Cornichons	2	2	2
Oil	2 tbsp	2 tbsp	2 tbsp
Lemon juice	1 tbsp	1 tbsp	1 tbsp
Sugar	1 tbsp	1 tbsp	1 tbsp
Salt	1 pinch	1 pinch	1 pinch
Boiled rice	1 cup	1 cup	1 cup
Cayenne pepper			

1. Drain the chanterelles in a sieve. Slice the cornichons. Combine the oil, lemon juice, sugar and salt. Transfer the chanterelles, cornichons and the rice into the sauce and mix well. Season to taste with cayenne pepper. Leave to marinate for a few hours.

SWEET CORN SALAD WITH BEANS AND CUCUMBER

INGREDIENTS	Metric	Imperial	American
Haricot beans, can	1 small	1 small	1 small
Sweet corn, can	1	1	1
Tomatoes	250 g	9 oz	9 oz
Cucumber	$\frac{1}{2}$	$\frac{1}{2}$	$\frac{1}{2}$
Onion	1	1	1
Shrimps	250 g	9 oz	9 oz
Wine vinegar	2 tbsp	2 tbsp	2 tbsp
Oil	3 tbsp	3 tbsp	3 tbsp
Salt			
Pepper			
Parsley, chopped			

1. Drain the beans and the sweet corn. Blanch the tomatoes, peel and seed them, then cut them into strips. Peel and finely slice the cucumber. Finely chop the onion. Mix the shrimps with the vegetables.

2. Combine the vinegar, oil and seasoning to make a dressing, pour over the salad and leave to marinate for 30 minutes. Then garnish with parsley and serve.

CHICORY SALAD

INGREDIENTS	Metric	Imperial	American
Chicory	500 g	1 lb	1 lb
Banana	1	1	1
Apples	2	2	2
Oranges	2	2	2
Lemon juice	4-6 tbsp	4-6 tbsp	4-6 tbsp
Yoghurt	1 carton	1 carton	1 carton
Soured cream	2 tbsp	2 tbsp	2 tbsp
Sugar	1 pinch	1 pinch	1 pinch

1. Cut the bitter tips out of the chicory, then wash the heads and cut them in slices. Peel and dice the fruit.

2. Combine the remaining ingredients to make a piquant dressing, spoon over the salad, mix and chill well before serving.

ORANGE SALAD 'IMPERIAL'

INGREDIENTS	Metric	Imperial	American
Oranges	2	2	2
Mushrooms, can	1 small	1 small	1 small
Asparagus, can	1 small	1 small	1 small
Mayonnaise	100 g	4 oz	4 oz
Salt			
Paprika			
Curry powder			
Yoghurt			
Lemon juice			
Brandy			
Lettuce leaves, marinated			
Toasted almond pieces	50 g	2 oz	$\frac{1}{2}$ cup

1. Peel, dice, then drain the oranges and reserve the juice. Slice the mushrooms, cut the asparagus into pieces and add to the oranges. Season the mayonnaise and add curry powder for flavouring. Stir in the

yoghurt, lemon juice and reserved juice from the oranges and the brandy and pour over the salad. Leave to chill, arrange on the lettuce leaves and sprinkle with the almonds.

BEAN SPROUT SALAD WITH CRABMEAT

INGREDIENTS	Metric	Imperial	American
Beansprouts	250 g	9 oz	9 oz
Green peas, frozen	1 small packet	1 small packet	1 small packet
Salt	1 pinch	1 pinch	1 pinch
Butter	a little	a little	a little
Crabmeat	250 g	9 oz	9 oz
Oil	2 tbsp	2 tbsp	2 tbsp
Lemon juice	1 tbsp	1 tbsp	1 tbsp
Soy sauce	1 tbsp	1 tbsp	1 tbsp
Ground ginger	1 pinch	1 pinch	1 pinch
Monosodium glutamate	1 tsp	1 tsp	1 tsp

1. Place the beansprouts in a bowl and pour boiling water over them. Leave for 5 minutes, then drain and pour cold water over them. Cook the peas until tender, season, then turn in melted butter. Leave to cool.

2. Combine the peas, beansprouts and the crabmeat. Whisk the oil with the lemon juice, soy sauce, ginger and monosodium glutamate and pour over the salad.

SPRING SALAD

INGREDIENTS	Metric	Imperial	American
Carrots	2	2	2
Kohlrabi	2	2	2
Cucumber	1 small	1 small	1 small
Tomatoes	250 g	9 oz	9 oz
Radishes	a few	a few	a few
Cress	50 g	2 oz	2 oz
Yoghurt	1 carton	1 carton	1 carton

Oil	1 tbsp	1 tbsp	1 tbsp
Vinegar	1 tbsp	1 tbsp	1 tbsp
Tomato ketchup	1 tbsp	1 tbsp	1 tbsp
Liquid	1 tbsp	1 tbsp	1 tbsp
Salt			
Cress, for garnishing	50 g	2 oz	2 oz

1. Peel and wash the carrots and kohlrabi, then grate them coarsely. Wash and slice the cucumber, tomatoes and radishes. Wash and drain the cress.

2. Combine the remaining ingredients to make a dressing, pour over the salad and toss well. Arrange the cress on a deep plate and place the salad on top.

DUTCH CAULIFLOWER SALAD

INGREDIENTS	Metric	Imperial	American
Cauliflower	1	1	1
Salted water			
Lemon juice	1 tbsp	1 tbsp	1 tbsp
Cheese (such as Chester)	125 g	$4\frac{1}{2}$ oz	$4\frac{1}{2}$ oz
Mixed pickles, jar	1 small	1 small	1 small
Tomatoes	3	3	3
Ham, slices	4	4	4
Mayonnaise	100 g	4 oz	4 oz
Curry powder			
Sugar			
Yoghurt	2 tbsp	2 tbsp	2 tbsp
Chives			

1. Cook the separated cauliflower in a little salted water until tender, drain, then sprinkle with lemon juice. Dice the cheese, mixed pickles, tomatoes and the ham and mix with the cauliflower. Add yoghurt to the mayonnaise together with curry powder and sugar to taste, fold under the salad and garnish with chopped chives.

WALDORF SALAD

INGREDIENTS	Metric	Imperial	American
Celeriac	300 g	11 oz	11 oz
Apples	300 g	11 oz	11 oz
Celery salt			
Juice of lemon	1	1	1
Sugar	1 tsp	1 tsp	1 tsp
Salad seasoning			
Mayonnaise	100 g	4 oz	4 oz
Walnuts	100 g	4 oz	1 cup

1. Peel, then finely grate the celeriac and the apples. Add lemon juice, sugar and seasoning and leave to marinate for 1 hour.

2. Mix the mayonnaise under the salad, stir in half the walnuts. Sprinkle the remaining nuts on top and serve.

PINEAPPLE-CELERY SALAD

INGREDIENTS	Metric	Imperial	American
Pineapple, can	1	1	1
Celery hearts, can	1	1	1
Lemon juice			
Hazelnuts, chopped	50 g	2 oz	$\frac{1}{2}$ cup
Single cream	125 ml	4 fl oz	$\frac{1}{2}$ cup
Pepper			
Salt			
Tomatoes			
Olives			
Parsley			

1. Cut the pineapple and celery into pieces of the same size and combine with the dressing, made by whisking lemon juice, nuts and cream together with a little pepper and salt. Garnish with tomatoes, olives and parsley. Leave to marinate for some time.

INFORMATION ON NUTRITIONAL VALUES

IMPORTANT FACTS ON CALORIES AND JOULES

Our daily food should be made up of a balanced combination of foods. One-sided nutrition is nearly as bad as being overweight.

To keep our body fit, it needs a daily intake of protein, fat and carbohydrates, and also minerals and vitamins — all in balanced amounts.

The ideal composition is as follows:
about 50% carbohydrates
about 30% fat
about 20% protein

You can calculate your ideal weight as follows:
170 cm high minus 100 = 70 kg minus 10% = 63 kg.

To keep this weight, you should eat no more than 40 calories per day per kilogramme.

Carbohydrates, fat, and protein are very important for providing energy.

Carbohydrates are contained mainly in pasta, potatoes, bread, pastries, sweets, honey and alcohol. If you eat too many carbohydrates this can lead to obesity, as superfluous carbohydrates are transformed into fat and stored in 'bulges'.

Fat is responsible for most of the calories in our food. If the body is given too much fat over a long period of time, it will be transformed into reserve. Therefore, eat no more than 80 g of fat per day; 'invisible' fat, e.g. in cheese (see our calory chart), is included in that amount. The average person eats 130 g per day!

Protein is found in rich supply in dairy products, meat (especially lean meat), fish, and eggs. Protein is an essential nutrient in any diet. It is important for creating cellular and tissue material. Both adolescents and adults need a certain amount of protein per day:

Adolescents up to 18 years	1.5 g per kg
Adults up to 65 years	1.0 g per kg
Adults over 65 years	1.2 g per kg

Become more figure conscious!
1) Be more aware and more selective in your choice of food.
2) Eating regularly and chewing food well will boost your metabolism.
3) Five meals a day are more sensible than three substantial meals —
they will make less demands on your body.
4) Serve a lot of fruit and vegetables every day — there are some ideas
in the recipe section.
5) Protein is of vital importance in our nutrition and is easily digestible.
It is the nutrient of our time, since we perform so little physical work.
6) The intake of fat should not exceed 75-80 g per day, and this includes
the invisible fat.
7) Reduce alcoholic and sweetened beverages.
8) Eating and drinking belong to life's pleasures — therefore arrange
your meals decoratively and take your time to enjoy them!

Energy values
In 1975, an international system was brought in that replaced calories as
the measure of energy value with Kilojoules.

Joule (calory) table
The figures indicate, unless otherwise stated, the joule (calory) value
per edible part of 100 g food.

Food	Protein g	Carbo-hydrates g	Fat g	Joule	Calories
Meat					
Mutton	15	—	32	1549	370
Veal	21	—	1	439	105
Beef	19	—	13	858	205
Pork	14	—	35	1653	395
Offal	17	1	6	552	132
Game					
Hare	22	—	3	519	124
Stag	21	—	3	514	123
Rabbit	21	—	8	699	167
Venison, leg of	21	—	1	444	106
Poultry					
Duck	18	—	17	1017	243
Goose	16	—	31	1523	364
Roasting chicken	21	—	6	602	144

Food	Protein g	Carbo- hydrates g	Fat g	Joule	Calories
Cold meats					
Ham	20	—	21	1180	282
Streaky bacon	9	—	65	2754	658
Butter	1	—	82	3160	755
Margarine	1	—	80	3140	750
Lard	—	—	100	3893	930
Oil	—	—	100	3893	930
Mayonnaise 50%	1	8	50	1946	465
Eggs	13	1	11	699	167
Egg yolk	16	—	32	1578	377
Egg white	11	1	—	226	54
Fruit yoghurt	4	14	0.5	335	80
Creamy yoghurt	10	13	10	766	183
250 g/9 oz/1½ cups carton	—	—	—	1915	457
Buttermilk	3	4	0.5	146	35
Low fat milk	3	5	2	209	50
Milk	3	5	3.5	267	64
Evaporated milk, 7.5%, 1 tbsp	7	10	7.5	573	137
Camembert cheese	22	2	13	941	225
Fish					
Cod	17	—	—	326	78
Eel	13	—	26	1251	299
Salmon	18	—	1	368	88
Trout	19	—	2	435	104
Vegetables					
Artichokes	2	12	—	251	60
Asparagus	2	3	—	83	20
Brussels sprouts	4	7	—	217	52
Carrots	1	7	—	146	35
Cauliflower	3	4	—	117	28
Celery	1	2	—	87	21

Cucumber	1	1	—	41	10
Curly endive	2	2	—	71	17
Haricot beans	2	5	—	138	33
Mushrooms	3	3	—	100	24
Onions	1	10	—	118	45
Peas	7	14	1	389	93
Peppers	1	5	—	117	28
Red, white, Savoy cabbage	2	4	—	108	26
Tomatoes	1	3	—	79	19

Fruit

Bananas	1	21	—	376	90
Grapes	1	17	1	309	74
Lemons	1	6	—	167	40
Oranges	1	9	—	226	54
Pineapple	1	13	—	238	57

Starchy foods

Bread, white	8	50	1	1088	260
Pasta	13	72	3	1632	390
Potatoes	2	19	1	355	85

Sweet spreads

Honey	—	81	—	1276	305
Jam	1	64	—	1075	257

Nuts

Almonds	18	17	54	2720	650
Hazelnuts	14	13	62	2888	690
Peanuts	27	19	47	2637	630

Beverages
Alcohol

Beer	1	4	4	200	48
Brandy	—	—	33	1017	243
Dessert wine	—	9	16	669	160
Light red wine	—	—	8	276	66
Liqueurs	—	31	29	1356	324
Spirits, 32Vol%	—	—	26	774	185
Whisky	—	—	35	1046	250

INDEX